i WAS THINKING...

Travels in the World of Ideas

For Noah & Liam —

Travel far & wide
in the world of
ideas.

PETER A. GILBERT

FOREWORD BY JAY PARINI

Peter Gilbert

i Was Thinking...

Travels in the World of Ideas

PETER A. GiLBERT
FOREWORD BY JAY PARINI

Published by
Wind Ridge Publishing, Inc.
Shelburne, Vermont 05482

i WAS THiNKiNG
Travels in the World of Ideas

Published by Wind Ridge Publishing, Inc.
P.O. Box 752
Shelburne, Vermont 05482

ISBN: 978-1-935922-11-7
Library of Congress: 2012937083

This volume is dedicated to my wife, Cindy Char;
our daughters, Carolyn and Julia; and my parents.

Contents

CHAPTER THREE

The Power and Pleasure of Poetry

CHAPTER FOUR

Robert Frost

CHAPTER FIVE
Vermont, These Green Hills and Silver Waters

Foreword

"Stay away from books," writes Peter Gilbert, "they have a long re-
cord of doing dangerous things, like changing lives." In his public
radio commentaries, Gilbert has been doing this year after year: drawing the listener close, and changing lives in the little ways that matter.
Now we have this elegant collection: *I Was Thinking... Travels in the
World of Ideas.*

I've been listening to these commentaries over the years, so it was
good to have them in hand as reading matter. Looking at them again,
I'm amazed by the range of Gilbert's interests, from politics to literature, from archaeology to American history, from baseball to philosophy. One can only marvel at the breadth of Gilbert's learning, the band-
width of his sensibility, which includes large quantities of humor as
well as pathos. He seems capable of taking up almost any subject that
attracts him, dwelling deeply there, and reporting back with insights
and memorable thoughts.

As director of the Vermont Humanities Council, he has done a
great deal to promote culture and civilized conversation in his home
state, and so it comes as no surprise that he writes often as well as
beautifully and sincerely about the wonders of this region that Robert
Frost called "north of Boston." Gilbert has become an anatomist of Vermont itself, its varied life and various seasons. Indeed, he notes in one
piece: "It's said that Vermont has six seasons: the usual four and mud
season, between winter and spring, and stick season between fall and
winter, when the leaves are mostly down and trees stand bare under
skies that are more often gray than blue. For many, stick season brings
with it a sense of loss; we cling to memories of bluer, greener days
before the frost was on the pumpkin."

This isn't just good writing. It's writing that tells us about our
lives, and that provides images to live by. Not surprisingly, Gilbert is not
only a lover of Robert Frost, the supreme poet of Vermont, but he is expert in talking about the poems in ways that make them freshly available to the general public. He seeks what Virginia Woolf once called

"the common reader."

Needless to say, he fully appreciates the true complications of Frost, a canny poet who once admitted to his readers that poetry is "the one acceptable way to say one thing and mean another." Gilbert looks at any number of poems here closely, including "The Road Not Taken," "The Silken Tent," and "Two Tramps in Mud Time." In each case, he reads between the lines as he reads the lines themselves, noticing what Frost said in quiet ways that might at first go unappreciated by the reader. In "Two Tramps," for instance, he describes the delicate balance of natural elements found in that first stanza: "I read the poem many times before I noticed that everything on that day is in perfect if fragile balance. For example, the weather is poised delicately between winter and spring." In his fine reading of this poem, he observes that Frost, at the end, fails to tell us whether or not he kept the pleasure of chopping the wood for himself or gave the work to these tramps who needed the work just to survive. Gilbert concludes: "Often what we want and need for ourselves is finely balanced with our moral obligation to others, as balanced as the weather on a lovely April day."

These little essays are miracles of balance, as the author finds exactly his point of purchase on the world, the place where meaning resides, almost hidden. He does so perfectly when he writes about "Reluctance," an early Frost poem with unusual depths and linguistic resources. It's a poem, as Gilbert tells us, about love. The poet apparently wrote the poem when he was only twenty and feared the loss of Elinor, the woman who eventually became his wife. Gilbert writes: "Like all great literature, this poem continues to resonate in my mind and helps me cope with whatever endings that life inevitably brings."

It was the great critic, Samuel Johnson, who reminded us: "The purpose of art is to help us better to enjoy our lives, or better to endure them." In these wise and passionate essays, Peter Gilbert would seem to concur with Johnson. He tries again and again to explain to us why literature matters, why thinking is better than not thinking, why understanding where we came from will help to know where we are headed. He records moments of perception, gleaned from history or literature, gleaned from living, and his recollections are worth saving.

—*Jay Parini, Middlebury College*

Introduction

Most of these short essays relate to the joys that can be found in the world of ideas, the power of language, and the importance of empathy, the examined and committed life, and what I'd call American idealism. In writing these pieces for broadcast on Vermont Public Radio and publishing them here, I have several goals in mind. I hope to connect the world of ideas with everyday life; to make academic subjects seem less distant—and not *academic* at all; to make history more engaging and more obviously relevant to both the present and our visions of the future; to make people curious and anxious to learn more; and to make poetry less daunting for many.

I hope the essays speak to the power of ideas and the pleasure of reading, and that they show that the world of ideas—the world of the humanities and books—is endlessly engaging, rewarding, and enjoyable. That world is open and accessible to all, formally educated and not, young and old. It is, largely, free. And one doesn't need a passport, save perhaps a library card, to explore it.

The world of ideas is not only satisfying; it's also important. And so finally, I hope to encourage thinking, to invite people to think in new ways and different directions. Increasingly, it seems, we are outsourcing the formation of our opinions to others—pundits, talking heads, columnists, and even radio commentators! Such people, if expert, wise, and reasonable, can provide valuable information, insight, and perspective, but their opinions should be used to form—and inform—our own. They should not be embraced uncritically.

For some years I've thought that reading is increasingly looked upon as too demanding, too low-tech, too labor intensive. Reading is harder than watching a video or listening to someone talking. It's certainly harder than sweeping a single finger lightly across a touch screen. It requires more sustained attention than the modern world encourages.

But the problem is bigger than that—because reading and thinking are closely related. We need to be on guard lest we tend to look at not just reading but also *thinking* as too demanding, too low-tech, and too labor intensive. In what appears to be a paradox, Americans may have become more opinionated and yet less confident in their capacity to think for themselves. Could that be in part because Americans are reading less? And engaging less with the world of ideas?

Thinking and Other Inherently Dangerous Activities

The Case for Literature

April 29, 2010

I read a startling commentary in *Education Week*, the key periodical in the country about K-12 education. It said that the National Council of Teachers of English was looking for volunteers for an ad hoc task force to gather evidence about why literature should continue to be taught in schools.

That's because there's a not unreasonable effort underway to establish common core measurable standards that would shape what's taught in English and Language Arts classes in U.S. schools. What's shocking to me is that, in light of that effort, someone would feel—perhaps with justification—that it's necessary to defend teaching literature. But experience has shown that knowledge and skills that aren't evaluated by the high-stakes tests that assess students' academic performance can quickly get squeezed out of the school schedule.

Perhaps the author of the commentary wanted to present arguments in favor of teaching literature that are themselves measurable because the only argument she makes is the compelling need to improve American students' poor reading scores. As she accurately points out, they are disappointingly, even alarmingly, low. She notes that the best way to make stronger readers is to have them read more, and the best way to do that is—hold on to your hats—to have them read books, not just articles or short snippets on the web. (Research shows that reading on the web hardly rises to the level of even skimming, and bears little resemblance to what's involved in reading a novel, biography, or history book.)

But the rationale for reading books in English class is not limited to the important goal of promoting strong reading skills. For generations reading literature has also been the way that American students have learned their country's history and world history, how they learned about morality (by reading about virtuous and not-so-virtuous people), how they learned about good and bad leaders, and how they learned about the dangers of pride, greed, and other human foibles.

The same should be true today. Moreover, reading books (both fiction and non-fiction) also teaches critical thinking skills—that is, the ability to analyze information from various sources and form conclusions for oneself. Long ago, some Englishman said that the purpose of education was to enable someone to tell when a person was speaking rot. I think that's a pretty good definition of critical thinking, and Lord knows, we are still in great need of the ability to tell when someone is speaking rot.

Reading literature also teaches, among other things, empathy: it puts us in another person's shoes, whether that person be Anne Frank, Holden Caulfield, or a conflicted young man named Hamlet. And certainly society could use a bit more empathy these days. Literature enlarges our lives, it gets us out of ourselves, and at the same time, it helps us see ourselves more clearly. In short, not only does literature make us better readers, it also makes us better citizens and employees, and most importantly, it helps us live our lives.

The Hazards of Reading

April 16, 2009

During National Library Week several years ago, I offered some surprising advice, especially coming from the head of the Vermont Humanities Council, which promotes literacy, reading, lifelong learning, and civic engagement. I warned people about something extremely dangerous—reading. Reading can lead to thinking, and there's no knowing where that can lead. It can encourage curiosity, and you know what curiosity did to the cat. It can lead to knowledge—even, over time, wisdom, but that won't get you on the cover of *Rolling Stone*. And it can be fun, but Lord knows, with all the troubles in the world today, levity is the last thing that's called for.

Let me give you three literary examples of the pernicious effects of reading. Ray Bradbury's 1953 novel *Fahrenheit 451* describes a future American society so hedonistic and anti-intellectual that critical thought through reading books is outlawed. If books are discovered, the firemen are called, and the volumes burned. Why? Because reading can be upsetting. Books can introduce you to disturbing ideas; they can challenge the status quo, or even your own convictions. Bradbury said that his novel wasn't about censorship, but about how television destroys interest in reading and leads to a sense that knowledge comprises mere factoids without context or significance.

Bradbury wasn't the only novelist who knew the dangers of reading. Cervantes, author of the very first novel, *Don Quixote*, knew it too. So I'd say that since Day One, novelists have been putting out products that are inherently dangerous to those who use them. Don Quixote, Cervantes' comic hero, is, you'll remember, a bit touched in the head. He mistakes windmills for monsters and his broken down old horse for a noble steed. What turned his head? Reading too many chivalric romances. And so, at the beginning of the novel, the curate and barber come into Don Quixote's library and burn countless volumes of romances.

Speaking of the pernicious influence of romances, Mark Twain absolutely hated Sir Walter Scott, the early-nineteenth-century English author of *Ivanhoe* and other historical novels that romanticized war and bygone days. Twain thought that Scott had such a large hand in forming the character of Southerners in this country that Scott was in great measure responsible for the Civil War. Twain asserted that "the Sir Walter disease" encouraged the South to be in love with "dreams and phantoms ... with decayed and degraded systems of government; with the sillinesses and emptinesses, sham grandeurs ... chivalries of a brainless and worthless long-vanished society" and with dueling, inflated speech, and social caste. That's why, in *The Adventures of Huckleberry Finn*, Twain has Huck (who romanticizes robbers and murderers) go on to a wrecked steamboat in the middle of a torrential rainstorm; there he happens upon three real-life robbers and murderers, and he witnesses their stark cruelty and the utter lack of honor among thieves. The name of the wrecked steamboat? "The Walter Scott."

My advice? Stay away from books—they might change your life, and hey, why mess with perfection?

Schweitzer on Thinking

May 31, 2011

I recently picked up the autobiography of Albert Schweitzer and was struck by how Schweitzer's concerns about the lack of thought or reason in society are as timely today as they were when he wrote them eighty years ago. Born in what was then the Alsace region of Germany in 1875, Albert Schweitzer was a Christian theologian, philosopher, organist devoted to the study of music by Bach, and physician who worked in West Africa in the early twentieth century. He won the Nobel Peace Prize in 1952 for his altruism, "reverence for life," and commitment to world brotherhood.

In his 1931 autobiography, *Out of My Life and Thought,* Schweitzer wrote that he was "in complete disagreement with the spirit of [his] age because it [was] filled with contempt for thought." A man of deep faith, he was nonetheless concerned about both the neglect of thought and society's mistrust of it. "The organized political, social, and religious associations of our time are at work convincing the individual not to develop his convictions through his own thinking but to assimilate the ideas they present to him. Any man who thinks for himself," he wrote, "is to them inconvenient and even ominous."

Schweitzer argued that society tries "to rob [modern man] of all confidence in his own thinking. He lives in an atmosphere of intellectual dependence…. [He's] forced into skepticism about his own thinking, so that he may become receptive to what he receives from authority." People soon conclude that they are not qualified to come to their own conclusions.

Schweitzer wrote that when we lose confidence in both our ability to think and the potential to arrive at the truth through thinking, then general skepticism develops. He asserted that those who promote such skepticism in order to confuse and control the populous believe that in time "men will come to accept as true whatever is forced upon them by authority and by propaganda."

But Schweitzer believed they are mistaken. "Whoever opens the sluices to let a flood of skepticism pour over the land," he wrote, "cannot assume that later he can stem the flood. Only a few of those who give up the search for truth will be so docile as to submit once and for all to official doctrine. The mass of people will... lose all desire for truth, finding themselves quite comfortable in a life without thought, driven... from one opinion to another."

I expect that Schweitzer is right that promoters of general skepticism can't necessarily control the beast they unleash, whether they are, as he said, organized political, social, religious—or, I would add commercial—associations. They can't necessarily control for long what the masses think. But that is of little comfort; after all, if skepticism is unchecked, then the mass of people live without thought, leaping from opinion to opinion when a more compelling sales pitch or a more attractive advocate comes along. That's hardly an attractive vision for any society. A healthy democracy requires that all its citizens, regardless of their opinions and beliefs, keep their brains attached.

Doubt and Conviction

September 16, 2003

The intolerance of extremism is running rampant. It's not just Al Qaeda. It's murders of doctors at abortion clinics. It's individuals like Timothy McVeigh, who saw himself as a modern-day John Brown and thought his attack on the Federal Building in Oklahoma City would inspire others to do likewise. It's in the Middle East, and so many other places. You can see it in the total confidence that some people at both extremes of political or ideological spectrums have in the rightness of their views, confidence that can become self-righteousness. Perhaps it was ever thus.

Robert F. Kennedy observed, "[w]hat is dangerous about extremists is not that they are extreme but that they are intolerant." That dangerous intolerance comes from their utter confidence in their means and ends.

In May of 1944, in the midst of World War II, New York City celebrated "I am an American Day" with speeches in Central Park. One speaker was Judge Learned Hand, a jurist so eminent that many called him the tenth Supreme Court Justice. He said, "The spirit of liberty is the spirit which is not too sure that it is right; the spirit of liberty is the spirit which seeks to understand the mind of other men and women ... which weighs their interests alongside its own without bias...."

How do we teach our children to have the courage of their convictions on the one hand, and, at the same time, to keep open to the possibility that they may be wrong? That is a difficult, even metaphysical, challenge.

You see that mindset in Abraham Lincoln. Lincoln was deeply, profoundly convinced that slavery was wrong and that the Union must be saved, and he gave his all for the cause. And yet he knew that the South, too, saw its cause as right. He does not judge the South. "It may seem strange," Lincoln observed in his second inaugural address, "that any men should dare to ask a just God's assistance in wringing their bread from the sweat of other men's faces, but let us judge not, that we be not judged."

Despite this uncertainty, Lincoln concludes that the North should pursue the war to a successful conclusion: "[W]ith firmness in the right, as God gives us to see the right, let us strive on to finish the work we are in...." Lincoln was a great president and great man because while wholly dedicated to his cause, he retained his humility.

The real world is not an ivory tower ethics seminar; it requires decisions—actions and reactions—often when there are no good choices. The challenge is to act out of one's deeply held convictions but not to lose that speck of humility—of doubt—that checks our intolerance, keeps us open to others' points of view, deters us from dehumanizing our enemies, and guards us against overstepping.

The Bystander Effect

March 13, 2006

On March 13, 1964, twenty-nine-year-old Kitty Genovese was brutally stabbed to death on the street near her home in Queens, New York. Thirty-eight neighbors heard her cries for help over a half-hour period, and none of them called the police. It wasn't so much her horrific murder that shocked the nation as it was the inaction of so many apparently normal, decent people. What has our society come to, people asked.

The event was taken to be an expression of alienated modern man's reluctance to get involved. But scientists concluded that it was also an example of the power of a group to influence individuals' opinions, attitudes, and actions—consciously or unconsciously. It's called the bystander effect, a psychological phenomenon that causes people to be less likely to intervene in an emergency when others are present than when they are alone. People don't act partly because they think someone else will act. There is a diffusion of personal responsibility.

In other cases of the bystander effect, when people are standing around watching a situation unfold, people's inaction causes others to not act as well because—here's the really disturbing part—their understanding of the nature and seriousness of the situation is influenced by how others react.

In the 1950s, psychology researcher Solomon Asch asked students to participate in a "vision test" comparing four straight lines on a card. Test-takers were asked to say which line was the longest and which lines were the same length. The differences in length were not subtle; the correct answers were obvious, but many participants were willing to change their answer when other students (who were actually working for the professor) argued for an incorrect answer. In other words, the expressed opinions of others—like the inaction of other bystanders—were enough to cause participants to doubt and deny the reality they saw right before their eyes.

This is scary stuff. Of course, we know that humans are social beings, emotional as well as rational. But to realize that our perception or understanding of reality itself is affected by the reactions of other people is enough to make the ground seem to shift beneath you.

What can we do about our tendency to be overly influenced by others? The most important thing is to be aware of that potential. Studies show that informing people about the bystander effect makes them more likely to help. It's also empowering to know that when we feel like we're the only person in a group who thinks a certain way, that's almost invariably not the case; it's just that no one's had the gumption to speak up or to stand up and act.

While we should remain open to other's opinions, we should also be appropriately skeptical of others' action or lack of it when it seems misguided; we should be dubious of assertions that fly in the face of experience. We need to retain the courage and energy to think, feel, and act for ourselves.

The Miracle of Written Language

July 28, 2009

Given all the activity around the four hundredth anniversary of Samuel de Champlain's coming to Vermont, I watched again a powerful movie about the interaction between French Jesuit missionaries and the Native peoples in 1634—when Champlain was Governor of New France. The movie, *Black Robe*, is interesting for many reasons, but in one scene, an Algonquin brave is talking with a French missionary. The priest is writing in his journal. The Indian asks him what he's doing, and he replies, "Making words."

"Words!" the Indian says. "You not speak!"

And the priest says, "I will show you. Tell me something I do not know."

The Algonquin thinks a moment and then says, "My woman's mother died in snow last winter."

The priest writes, then walks over and shows his journal to another Frenchman, who reads, "Last winter Chomina's wife's mother died in the snow."

The Indian is dumbstruck, absolutely astonished by this apparently miraculous silent conveying of detailed information.

We usually take it for granted, but written language really is amazing. In spite of its problematic stereotypical characterization of Native Americans, I like the scene in the movie because it conveys, with great force and novelty, something of the power of writing and reading.

There's a similar scene I like as well, in another, albeit lesser movie. It reminds me that written symbols on a page stand for words, and they, in turn stand for ideas; they can be stored indefinitely, then decoded, and turned into sound.

In *The 13th Warrior* Antonio Banderas plays a diplomat from Baghdad to northern Europe in the year 922. He joins a dozen Norse warriors to go fight a terrifying foe. At one point, one of the Norsemen, dressed in crude clothes and furs, asks the elegantly dressed Banderas, "You can draw sounds?"

"Yes," he replies. "I can draw sounds. And I can speak them back."

"Show me," says the illiterate European.

And so Banderas writes in Arabic in the sand.

How many of us would think of describing writing as "drawing sounds" and reading as "speaking the drawings back"?

Toward the end of the movie, when one of the valiant but illiterate warriors is mortally wounded, he points out that he is absolutely impoverished. But, he says, "A man might be thought wealthy if someone were to draw his deeds, that he might be remembered." He wants, of course, the Persian to write the history of his bravery, and of course, Banderas does.

It really is miraculous to be able to know words, thoughts, and feelings of men and women long dead. It is a kind of immortality. And what a great thing it is to help people learn to read—whether they be very young children or adults who, for any of a million reasons, never learned how.

Walden

September 30, 2004

In 1854 one of the most important books in American letters was published—*Walden*, by Henry David Thoreau. If there were one book that best embodies the spirit of the humanities, it very well might be *Walden*. Of course, no one book can encompass all those subjects that speak to what it means to be human: history, literature, ethics, philosophy, the study of religion and art, and the like. But *Walden* comes close because, as he himself writes, Thoreau went to live at Walden Pond because he wanted to live deliberately. And living deliberately is at the core of the humanities. They are about being thoughtful and reflective, living what Socrates called the examined life.

Nothing promotes thoughtfulness more than reading—except, perhaps, stillness and silence. Thoreau was good at both: he read and borrowed abundantly from other authors, and by removing himself from society for a time, he was sure to experience life as it was happening—to think and feel for himself. Thoreau called Walden Pond the "earth's eye; looking into which the beholder measures the depth of his own nature." If Walden Pond is Thoreau's mirror and means by which he comes to know himself, the humanities are the universal tools of self-reflection and self-knowledge.

In seeking to live deliberately, Thoreau took his own advice to "Simplify, simplify." By simplifying our lives, we're more able to remember what's really important and to connect with what Nobel Laureate William Faulkner called "the old verities and truths of the heart, the old universal truths ... love and honor and pity and pride and compassion and sacrifice." Only that, he said, is the stuff of good literature, and good lives.

"I went to the woods because I wished to live deliberately," Thoreau wrote, "to front only the essential facts of life, and see if I could not learn what it had to teach, and not, when I came to die, discover that I had not lived." One need not be a back-to-the-lander or even a fan of *Walden* to benefit from the spirit of that book, a century and a half young this year. As we go through life, we all need to keep in the forefront of our minds the fundamental themes of the human experience that Faulkner lists, because at joyful births and tearful deaths, those are the things that we think of. It would be a shame indeed if, as Thoreau writes, when it comes time to die, we discover that we haven't lived.

Twenty Centuries of Epiphanies

January 5, 2005

"The Twelve Days of Christmas" is a familiar song, but many don't know what the Twelve Days of Christmas are. They are December 25th through January 5th. The next day, January 6th, is called Epiphany, or Twelfth Night. The word epiphany means "a showing forth." In Western churches, Epiphany remembers the coming of the wise men, or Magi, bearing three gifts for the Christ child. Their visit is said to "reveal" Jesus to the world as the incarnate Christ. That would make the wise men's finding of the Christ child the first and ultimate epiphany.

Shakespeare entitled a play *Twelfth Night*, and some scholars believe that the romantic comedy was first performed for Queen Elizabeth I at Whitehall on Twelfth Night, January 6, 1601.

In the secular twentieth century, epiphanies had special, albeit not sacred, meaning for James Joyce, author of *A Portrait of the Artist as a Young Man*, *Ulysses*, and *Finnegans Wake*. For Joyce, epiphany meant a sudden revelation of the truth or essence of a thing. It refers to a moment of insight or understanding in which one understands the essential whatness of a thing, when "the soul of the commonest object...seems to us radiant." It means, in short, a moment of truth, understanding, discovery, or awareness.

Epiphanies are at the center of Joyce's literary works. His collection of short stories called *Dubliners* was, for him, a series of fifteen epiphanies written to let Irish people take "one good look at themselves." Scholars argue that *Dubliners* reveals what Joyce considered the essence of the entire city of Dublin: paralysis. It's no wonder, then, that while Joyce wrote largely about Dublin, he lived all of his creative years in continental Europe.

At one point, one of Joyce's characters, the largely autobiographical Stephen Hero, overhears just a snippet of conversation between a young man and woman, but Stephen found in those few words something transcendent. Joyce writes,

> This triviality made him think of collecting many such moments together in a book of epiphanies. By an epiphany he meant a sudden spiritual manifestation, whether in the vulgarity of speech or of gesture or in a memorable phase of the mind itself. He believed that it was for the man of letters to record these epiphanies with extreme care, seeing that they themselves are the most delicate and evanescent of moments.

Joyce said that epiphanies contain what Thomas Aquinas considered the three requisites of beauty: wholeness, harmony, and radiance. That's why Joyce found epiphanies so compelling—because they are beautiful and the very embodiments of truth revealed.

Where do you find epiphanies today? They are out there, but you have to look and choose to recognize them.

Making Time for Reading

September 3, 2003

E ach year when Labor Day has come and gone, I usually feel as if I've only made a dent in my summer reading. The stack of books I've been wanting to get to is still a big one.

The truth is that any season is perfect for reading. But there's the familiar dilemma, "Where will I ever find the time to read?" The answer is the same answer that Robert Frost gave when asked when he found time to write: "Like a sneak I stole some of it, like a man I seized some of it, and I had a little in my tin cup."

So here are some ways to fit more books into your busy life:

Read more than one book at once. Sometimes you feel like a sweet snack, other times something salty. The same idea applies with books. And if you're reading several at once, it's more likely one will be near at hand.

Don't finish books you don't like. There won't be a test.

Use a bookmark so it's easy to pick up where you left off. Or, if the book is yours and inexpensive, gently place it face down with the pages open to where you stopped reading. You'll be more likely to pick it up again.

If the arrival of a magazine provokes in you an exasperated, burdened sense of "more to read," let the subscription expire, and turn to the stack of books you have waiting for you.

Carry a book with you. Read while you're waiting—for the doctor, for your child, for an oil change.

Go to the library. People who are dieting should stay out of chocolate shops. People who want to encourage themselves to read should go to a library. They are chocolate shops for would-be readers.

Make conscious choices about watching TV. Instead of channel

surfing, read a TV schedule: if nothing interesting is listed, don't turn on the TV to check. When your favorite TV show is over, turn the tube off before the next lame show begins. (I know, easier said than done, but how many times do you or I have to regret spending an hour watching junk?) Hide your TV, or move it to a less prominent place: Out of sight, out of mind.
Finally, don't wait until you feel you have the time to read a whole book (which is never). Just begin.

There will always be more demands on our time than we can meet. By being deliberate about how we use our time, we make time for those things that matter most. As author Annie Dillard has observed, "How we spend our days is, of course, how we spend our lives."

Extraordinary Knowing

March 31, 2008

I'm a big fan of used bookstores as well as libraries, and so I was delighted to find a fascinating book amidst the miscellaneous volumes on the for-sale shelf at a public library. It gave my family and me a lot to think about.

The book, published in 2007, is called *Extraordinary Knowing: Science, Skepticism, and the Inexplicable Powers of the Human Mind* by the late Elizabeth Lloyd Mayer. I bought it for a few bucks because it related to a family dinner table conversation we had had just a week before. We were discussing whether we believed in ghosts. In short, the conclusion of several of us at least was that we weren't so sure about ghosts, but we did believe that the human mind had remarkable abilities to understand and even communicate across great distances— abilities that science does not now understand. Just because frauds and charlatans abound does not mean there's nothing to the countless credible incidents of extraordinary knowing whether they're called ESP, telepathy, intuitive knowing, paranormal phenomena, mind-matter anomalies, or distant viewing.

The book caught my eye in part because the cover noted that it contained forewords by Freeman Dyson, one of the world's most eminent theoretical physicists, and renowned psychologist Carol Gilligan, who has specialized in women's moral development. Their essays, which I read standing at the library checkout counter, assured me that the book wasn't just bunk.

Professor Dyson, in short, puts forth the hypothesis that ESP is real but belongs to a mental universe that is too fluid and evanescent to fit within the rigid protocols of controlled scientific testing. He doesn't claim that the hypothesis is true, only that it is consistent with the evidence and worthy of consideration.

These anomalous phenomena relate to learning across the board, including, for example, the holistic theories of Gestalt psychology; complementarity in physics, in which two descriptions of nature may both be valid but cannot be observed simultaneously; and the mind-blowing notion in quantum physics of entanglement, which has confirmed that an electron in Tokyo that was once related to an electron now in London appears to compensate instantaneously for a change in spin of the London electron. Could that have something to do with how a person in Tokyo could know what someone in London is thinking?

Professor Gilligan accurately calls Mayer's book an invitation to think about the inexplicable powers of the human mind. It's exciting—terrifying, actually—to consider such paradigm-shattering notions. It's a personal and intellectual challenge to be open to the implications of countless credible examples of anomalous knowing that we can't explain. We know that the scientific method is committed to proof. But, the author observes, if you have to discount significant amounts of scientifically gathered data because they're inconsistent with your world view, you may, in fact, not be a careful scientist, but rather one blinded by that world view. After all, as Mayer notes, they laughed at Galileo, too. It just may be, as Hamlet tells his friend Horatio, that there are more things in heaven and earth than are dreamt of in your philosophy.

Learning Vocabulary

December 16, 2009

Years ago, when I was teaching high school English, my students studied vocabulary words every week, as most high school students still do. But I knew full well that studying word lists didn't necessarily mean that the words would be learned, let alone become part of the students' active vocabulary. I admitted to them that word lists were not, in fact, the best way to increase their vocabularies.

I argued that there were three kinds of words: words you use and know what they mean, words that are familiar but you don't actually know what they mean, and words that are entirely unfamiliar—words that you don't think you've ever heard. The best way to increase one's vocabulary, I would assert, is to focus on the middle group of words: words that are familiar when you hear them, but, in fact, you don't know what they mean. If you've heard a word used, you're far more likely to remember its meaning and use it yourself than some word that's totally foreign to you.

Sometimes a familiar word that we don't know is part of a well-known phrase. And so once we know the word's meaning, we're more likely to remember it. For example, the Declaration of Independence talks of "certain unalienable rights." And so if you don't know what unalienable means, but you look it up, you'll probably remember that it means that the rights cannot be given or taken away. My recent favorite is the title of a new James Bond movie, *Quantum of Solace*. There are two not-too-familiar words, meaning a certain amount of comfort or easing of grief.

Of course, some words you've never heard before are so odd they're funny, and therefore their meanings are memorable if you go to the trouble of looking them up. "Borborygmus" has long been a favorite of mine. It means loud gastronomical rumblings—those embarrassing stomach growls before lunch. And there's "snood," a bag-like hairnet worn by women in the 1930s and '40s. I only know the word because Bing Crosby uses it in the movie *White Christmas*; because the word is weird, I looked it up. Listen for it this year when you watch that "Vermonty" holiday film.

Admittedly, increasing your vocabulary by learning the meaning of familiar words works best over a number of years, not cramming for the SATs. It also requires both that you notice when you bump into a word you don't know, and that you look it up. That takes a little extra effort.

Perhaps the greatest benefit of this approach to learning words is that you become more attentive to words you hear or read that you don't know, rather than unconsciously or consciously filtering them out. It's that greater awareness that, over time, causes you to learn more words and enjoy words more.

Aren't Rhetorical Questions Odd?

August 19, 2009

R hetorical questions are odd things, aren't they? I mean, don't they just make it harder for people to understand each other? Why can't we communicate in a more straightforward manner? Wouldn't that be simpler? Don't we do it just for rhetorical effect, because it sounds compelling and persuasive?

Intimidation is part of their effectiveness, isn't it? I mean, you don't really want to argue with someone who wants and expects wordless agreement, do you? And don't rhetorical questions set up a psychic "with us or against us" divide between those people intelligent enough to agree with the speaker and all those other, poor benighted souls?

Why do we continue to make statements in the form of questions? Wouldn't you think that we'd know better by now? Do you think it's "the Jeopardy effect"? Have we watched that TV show so often that we're now sure to state not only our answer in the form of a question, but also our statements? Has American culture really been reduced to that? What will become of us? Who knows?

But it's been ever thus, hasn't it? I mean, what does it say about our country that our national anthem, "The Star-Spangled Banner," written nearly 200 years ago, begins with two rhetorical questions and ends with a third?

> Oh, say can you see by the dawn's early light
> What so proudly we hailed at the twilight's last gleaming?
> Whose broad stripes and bright stars thru the perilous fight,
> O'er the ramparts we watched were so gallantly streaming?

And who can forget that stirring last line?

Oh, say does that star-spangled banner yet wave
O'er the land of the free and the home of the brave?

But it isn't just Americans, is it? Have you noticed how the English have the annoying habit of adding the words, "isn't it?" or "aren't they?" at the end of a sentence in an attempt to turn even the most dubious statements into unassailable assertions? Well, I mean, doesn't it make you want to throttle them?

Why is it that parents, too, tend to speak in rhetorical questions? "What in the world were you thinking? Have you lost your mind? Did you not hear what I just said? Do you think that money grows on trees? Do you expect these dishes to wash themselves? Who do you think you are, young lady? Whom do you think you're talking to? Where do you think you're going? How many times do I have to say it?"

When will we ever learn? But, hey, we don't have to take everything too seriously, now do we?

Lost Correspondence

November 27, 2007

During World War II, in 1943, a Japanese soldier at the front in Burma wrote a postcard to a friend in Nagasaki. The soldier died a year later, but his postcard was found by an American soldier. It was passed along through generations, and eventually landed in the hands of a Japanese exchange student who arranged to have it delivered to the intended recipient. He was then eighty years old, and he said that he was overwhelmed to have this connection with his late friend, sixty-four years later.

It's a moving story, and it caused me to think of incidences of lost and undelivered letters in works of literature. For the great American novelist Herman Melville, there was something deeply moving, deeply poignant, about letters that don't get delivered—human communication that goes awry. Both his masterpiece, *Moby Dick*, and his famous novella, *Bartleby, the Scrivener*, involve letters from loved ones that never reach their intended recipient. In both stories, that profound human desire to connect with others is frustrated and futile.

Melville seems to see post office mail sorters as especially alienated souls. In *Moby Dick,* the narrator, Ishmael, writes that his goal of systematically setting forth everything about whales is such "a ponderous task [that] no ordinary letter-sorter in the Post-office is equal to it. To grope down into the bottom of the sea after them," he writes, "... is a fearful thing."

Later, Ishmael explains that, "Every whale-ship takes out a goodly number of letters for various ships, whose delivery to the persons to whom they may be addressed, depends upon the mere chance of encountering them on the four oceans. Thus, most letters never reach their mark; and many are only received after attaining an age of two or three years or more."

Ishmael goes on to describe how his ship, *The Pequod*, received a letter from another vessel it happened to meet at sea: "[The envelope] was sorely tumbled, damp, and covered with a dull, spotted, green mould, in consequence of being kept in a dark locker of the cabin. Of such a letter, Death himself might well have been the post-boy."

The letter was from the wife of a sailor on *The Pequod* who had just recently died.

"'Poor fellow! poor fellow! and from his wife,' sighed one of the sailors."

We see the same theme in Melville's story, *Bartleby, the Scrivener: A Story of Wall-street*, written in 1853, two years after *Moby Dick*. That story should make us grateful for cards and letters delivered, for human connections successfully made. It tells about a successful Wall Street lawyer and the odd, alienated man he hires to copy legal documents. Increasingly, when Bartleby is asked to do something, he replies, "I would prefer not to."

After Bartleby's death, the narrator hears a rumor about Bartleby's past: apparently he'd been a clerk in the Dead Letter Office in Washington. The story ends with this poignant paragraph and final words:

> Dead letters! does it not sound like dead men? Conceive a man by nature and misfortune prone to a pallid hopelessness, can any business seem more fitted to heighten it than that of continually handling these dead letters and assorting them for the flames? For by the cart-load they are annually burned. Sometimes from out the folded paper the pale clerk takes a ring: the finger it was meant for, perhaps, moulders in the grave; a bank-note sent in swiftest charity: he whom it would relieve, nor eats nor hungers any more; pardon for those who died despairing; hope for those who died unhoping; good tidings for those who died stifled by unrelieved calamities. On errands of life, these letters speed to death.
>
> Ah Bartleby! Ah humanity!

The True Meaning of Philanthropy

December 6, 2011

When most of us think of philanthropists, we think of wealthy people who give a lot of money to charity, like Andrew Carnegie and Bill Gates. But the real meaning of philanthropy is found in the roots of the word itself.

The word comes from two Greek words: *philein*, meaning to love, and *anthropos* (as in anthropology), meaning humankind. And so philanthropy means love of humanity. That's really who a philanthropist is—one who acts out of love for humankind.

Author George McCully argues that the Greek mythological figure Prometheus might be considered the first philanthropist, even though he didn't really exist in the flesh. Prometheus was the mythical Titan said to have created humankind out of clay. But initially, those humans were without any knowledge or skills; they were brutish animals who lived in darkness in caves. Zeus, the king of the Greek gods, decided to destroy them. But Prometheus, because of his humanity-loving nature, steals fire from Mount Olympus and gives it to the humans. Imagine how great the gift of fire would be to humans who didn't have it to cook food, to protect and warm themselves, to illuminate the darkness, or to gather around with others in community. This mythical fire came to symbolize knowledge and skill—all that constitutes civilization.

With the gift of fire, Prometheus gave humans hope and justified their optimism. As McCully points out, the two gifts are complementary. With fire, optimism is justified, and optimism motivates people to use their new abilities to better the human condition. It follows that what separates humans from other animals is not opposable thumbs, or even language, but culture—civilization—the knowledge and skills that enable us to understand and improve our situation. That's what philanthropists do; they strive to better the human condition and help people achieve their potential.

I like the notion of philanthropists being people, wealthy or not, who act out of a loving desire to better the human condition. I also like McCully's observation that Cicero and other Romans translated the Greek word *philanthropia* into Latin as *humanitas*, in the sense of caring about and nourishing human potential. And so it is that history, literature, and other areas of thought that help us understand ourselves better have come to be called the Humanities, and are central to that lifelong process of understanding and bettering the human condition.

Most of all, I like the notion that if philanthropy is not about giving money, but rather about acting out of love for humankind, then philanthropy can be hugely positive, even transformative, for the donor as well as the recipient. That's because in giving, donors grow more into their own human potential; they grow in generosity and understanding. And if we give not until it hurts but rather until it feels good, then we tend to do it more. Now obviously, donating to a charity at the end of the year will not make you a saint or mahatma; but thinking humbly of yourself as a philanthropist, even one of modest means—as a person who acts and gives out of love for humankind—well, that's probably at least a step in the right direction.

2

The Past
Isn't Past

Footprints in the Serengeti

July 17, 2009

The flat, dry savanna of East Africa stretched away to the horizon in every direction, and there I stood on the side of a straight, gravel road, with my backpack on the ground beside me. Terrific, I thought. Not the most promising place to hitchhike. More to settle my nerves than to quench my thirst, I got my water bottle out of my pack, took a swig, and put my hat on to keep the strong equator sun off. As it turned out, it was just a half-hour before a country bus laden with luggage and Maasai locals came by, picked me up, and took me west to the Serengeti Plains.

I was in northern Tanzania, and had just visited Oldupai Gorge. There, in 1959, archeologist Mary Leakey set out in the morning to explore a part of the gorge where rains had caused significant erosion earlier in the year. Her husband, Louis Leakey, was in bed with the flu. First, she saw, sticking out of the ground, a fossilized bone, part of the bone that's just below the ear. She looked further, and gently brushing some dry earth away, saw two large teeth—definitely hominid.

She hurried back to camp to tell Louis, who rose from his sick bed to investigate. Eventually, 400 bone fragments were found, and over time, Mary was able to reconstruct the skull she'd unearthed. It was 1.7 million years old.

It was big news: the discovery demolished the then-prevailing notion that humankind's origin was either East Asian or even European. It meant that hominids had been living in Africa far longer than anyone had imagined, it contributed to the notion that Africa was the cradle of humankind, and it spurred important research worldwide.

Since that exciting day, older fossils have been found, but the discovery remains important. One of Mary Leakey's later discoveries, about 25 miles from Oldupai, was a fossilized trail of footprints of three small-brained apes, two walking upright side by side, the third follow-ing in one of their footsteps. You see their path in the volcanic ash for nearly eighty feet, and you see where, three and a half million years ago, something caused the smallest of them to stop and turn around for a moment before continuing on its way.

More recently, our teenage daughter has spent three summers just a hundred miles east of Oldupai Gorge volunteering at a high school for AIDS orphans. The school was also just 75 miles from the slopes of Mt. Kilimanjaro, where I taught another summer thirty-seven years before.

My footprints in the ochre African dust are long gone, but my memories and love for the region and its people are as well preserved as any fossil. And it seems that the place has made just as lasting an impression on our daughter.

The Mnemonic March of England's Kings and Queens

June 24, 2009

Years ago, an English friend and I drove a British Army Land Rover from the Arctic Ocean in very northern Canada south, back to civilization. It was a long and beautiful drive, and to pass the time, he taught me a little poem that tells you all the kings and queens of England in order, from William the Conqueror in 1066 to the reigning Queen of England today, Elizabeth II.

The poem I memorized is a wonderful mnemonic device, and it goes like this:

Willie, Willie, Harry, Stee ...

(That would be William the First, who was William the Conqueror; then William the Second, Henry the First, and then King Steven. Got the idea?)

Willie, Willie, Harry, Stee
Harry, Dick, John, Harry Three
One, Two, Three Neds, Richard Two
Henry Four, Five, Six, then who?
Edward Four, Five, Dick the Bad,
Harrys twain, and Ned the Lad,
Mary, Bess, James the Vain,
Charlie, Charlie, James again.
William and Mary, Anna Gloria,
Four Georges, William, and Victoria,
Edward Seven and Georgie Five,
Edward, George, and Bess Alive.

Who knows how we'll finish the poem when or if Charles, the current Prince of Wales, becomes King Charles the Third, or his older son becomes King William the Fifth?

Of course, there's a lot of English history condensed into that brief list of names, beginning with William the Conqueror, the Norman invader of England who defeated Harold at the Battle of Hastings in 1066, a story illustrated by the magnificent Bayeux Tapestry. There's "Dick the Bad": that's Richard III, whom Shakespeare made out to be a villain. Even the great (and late in life, hugely overweight) Henry VIII gets only a slight reference in the poem as one of the "Harrys twain." His daughter, Queen Elizabeth I, the long-reigning monarch of the glorious English Renaissance, including Shakespeare's day, and the Virgin Queen, in whose honor the Commonwealth of Virginia was named—even she, here, is simply "Bess." And King George III, the long-reigning king whom the American colonies revolted against in 1776, is just one of "four Georges" in a row shortly before Queen Victoria.

All this came to mind because five hundred years ago, on June 24, 1509, Henry VIII was crowned king. Without him, we wouldn't have the inspiring movie *A Man for All Seasons*, which tells the story of Thomas More, who feeling that integrity was worth dying for, stood up to Henry VIII when the King wanted to get a divorce and remarry. We wouldn't have the Church of England, and we wouldn't have that other mnemonic device about the fate of his six wives: "divorced, beheaded, died; divorced, beheaded, survived." Now if only there was an easy way to remember how to spell mnemonic.

The Richard III Society

August 21, 2006

You know those notices of loving remembrance published in newspapers, usually near the obituaries? Well, I saw one remarkable "In Memoriam" notice in the August 22 edition of *The New York Times*. It read, "PLANTAGENET - Richard. Remember before God, Richard III, King of England, and those who fell in Bosworth Field, having kept the faith, 22 August 1485." And then it gave the website of the Richard III Society, which I learned is dedicated to a reassessment of Richard III's reputation.

Members of the society, whose royal patron, by the way, is the current Duke of Gloucester, believe that Richard III is victim of one of the earliest character assassinations in English history.

Richard's bad reputation today stems largely from Shakespeare's play, *Richard III*. Relying on Tudor historians, including Thomas More, Shakespeare portrayed Richard as the wicked, hunchbacked uncle who murdered the two princes in the Tower of London. We know him from the stage and the printed page, from the movie version with Laurence Olivier, and from Richard Dreyfuss in *The Goodbye Girl*. The Richard III Society acknowledges that Shakespeare's play is beautifully written and that the Bard's smiling villain proves fascinatingly compelling. But, they argue, a compelling yarn is not necessarily accurate history.

They believe that "many features of the traditional accounts of the character and career of Richard III are neither supported by sufficient evidence nor reasonably tenable." Most medieval historians agree at least that Richard's guilt in the murder of the young princes in the Tower, as well as other crimes, is unclear. And it's unlikely that he was physically deformed; it is more likely that Shakespeare used physical deformity as a visible and outward manifestation of an inner, moral deformity.

Whatever the truth, why did Richard get such a bad rap? The short answer is that Shakespeare was writing plays during the reign of Elizabeth I, granddaughter to the exiled Henry Tudor, whose army invaded England, and defeated and killed Richard. Henry Tudor became Henry VII. His son was Henry VIII, who was Elizabeth's father. Obviously, if you write plays about the Queen's ancestors, you'd better be complimentary and certainly not cast any doubts on her right to the throne.

But what are we to think of this memorial ad and the efforts of the Richard III Society? Is it admirable work in pursuit of accurate historical understanding or an example of charming English eccentricity?

Its Royal Patron writes that the purpose of the Society "derives from the belief that the truth is more powerful than lies—a faith that even after all these centuries, the truth is important. It is proof of our sense of civilized values that something as esoteric and as fragile as reputation is worth campaigning for."

And I ask myself how I'd feel if I knew that 500 years from now history would remember a decent leader in the twentieth or twenty-first century as a murdering scoundrel, or, conversely, if a scoundrel of a leader would be remembered as honorable.

King James's Masterpiece

June 9, 2011

The creation of the King James Bible is something of a miracle. In 1604, England's new King, James I, convened a conference at Hampton Court to discuss matters of church and state. Out of the conference came a hugely ambitious project—a new English translation of the Bible—supposedly to deal with problems that the Puritans and other factions within the Church of England had with existing translations. Whatever the Puritans' concerns, King James wanted a translation that emphasized and celebrated (not surprisingly) kingship, order, and authority—a translation in which notions of godly majesty and kingly majesty merge.

It took seven years and about fifty men working in six committees or "companies." Two of the committees met in Oxford, two in Cambridge, and two in London; each group was assigned a number of books of the Bible to translate. Following the King's express instructions, each member of each committee translated every passage, and then the committee met together to produce a single, best text. When a committee had finished a book of the Bible, it was sent to the other five committees for their review, and then, finally, a general meeting worked to assure a unified text.

The notion of making a literary and religious masterpiece by committee—indeed six committees—sounds ludicrous, but amazingly, the effort proved a triumph. It produced a translation that might be considered one of the greatest works in the English language: elegant, eloquent, powerful, and poetic, and embodying the scholars' scrupulous care for accuracy, meaning, and nuance. Adam Nicolson tells this compelling story in his book, wonderfully entitled *God's Secretaries, The Making of the King James Bible*.

The language of the King James Bible seems today lofty and

old-fashioned. In fact it was archaic-sounding even when it was first published in 1611, four hundred years ago. Nicolson says that the "grandeur of phrasing and the deep slow music of its rhythms were conscious embodiments of regal glory." The translators referred to Greek, Hebrew, Latin, and Aramaic texts as well as other translations of the Bible, particularly one produced by a single man, William Tyndale, about eighty years earlier. But even Tyndale didn't hit every note just right, and where appropriate, King James' translators opted for other words or phraseology.

Nicolson contrasts the language of the King James Bible with that of not only Tyndale's translation but also the New English Bible, published in 1970. What was wanted in 1970, he explains, was not antiquated language, but "timeless" prose, an accessible text that conveyed a "sense of reality." The result, Nicolson argues, was the banal language of the memo, a style that made the Bible's extraordinary content sound ordinary, even mundane.

In contrast, the language of the King James Bible, Nicolson argues, was both touching and at the same time majestic. And it was that "touching majesty" that in turn made possible the inspiring language of some of the greatest speeches we know—including speeches by Lincoln, Kennedy, and King.

Anti-Intellectualism in American Life

October 5, 2009

In his 1964 Pulitzer Prize-winning classic *Anti-Intellectualism in American Life*, the distinguished historian Richard Hofstadter explores that fascinating theme in our culture, which, he notes, is older than the nation itself. His analysis is as thought provoking today as it was when it was first published. The roots of anti-intellectualism in this country are many and complex, but Hofstadter emphasizes four: the values and culture of democracy, egalitarianism, business, and evangelicalism.

First and foremost, he asserts that anti-intellectualism is rooted in our country's democratic institutions and egalitarian sentiments. He examines the Jacksonian movement, which, he says, was spurred by a distrust of expertise, a dislike of centralization, a desire to uproot the entrenched classes, and the fundamental notion that crucial governmental functions are actually simple enough to be performed by the average citizen. During the 1828 presidential campaign, Andrew Jackson was seen as a man of the people, a man of action, someone who had, according to Jacksonian literature, "practical common sense . . . more valuable than all the acquired learning of the sage." In contrast, the learning of his more intellectual opponent, incumbent John Quincy Adams, was seen as a detriment. Jackson beat Adams in a landslide.

Hofstadter argues that the world of business also plays a role here. Americans have long prided themselves as being doers: builders of bridges and railroads, conquerors of a continent—a practical people, energetic, ambitious, impatient. Even back in the early 1800s, French historian Alexis de Tocqueville noted that the emphasis in American business on constant action put a premium on quick decisions, the rough and ready mind, and the intuitive leader over the deliberative, thoughtful approach. Americans have long been more fond of the so-called "wisdom of intuition," which is deemed to be natural or God-given, than we are of rationality and learning, which are cultivated and artificial.

Another root of anti-intellectualism, according to Hofstadter, is our religious history. Evangelical religion, he argues, relates more to the heart than it does to the rational mind. Over time, he asserts, "the Puritan ideal of the minister as an intellectual and educational leader was steadily weakened in the face of the evangelical ideal of the minister as a popular crusader and exhorter." Forty-five years ago, he wrote, "in modern [American] culture the evangelical movement has been the most powerful carrier of this kind of religious anti-intellectualism."

Hofstadter acknowledges that those who are fearful of intellect have cause to be: thinking and intellect are, in a way, dangerous. If we start thinking deeply about things, he notes, there's no way to know what facets of the status quo or one's own deeply held assumptions might be challenged, including political, social, economic, religious, and scientific sacred cows. A threatening prospect indeed.

America's Tenacious Regional Differences

June 23, 2011

I'm often struck by just how dissimilar attitudes and opinions are in different regions of our country. One can actually map the dominant attitudes around the country regarding government, taxes, liberty, religion, gender, violence, and many other cultural characteristics. And those differences have sustained themselves for a very long time despite the homogenizing tendencies of mass media and a highly mobile society.

In 1989 historian David Hackett Fischer published a fascinating and hugely ambitious book entitled *Albion's Seed*. It discusses four different waves of immigration from England to what is now the United States. Each wave came from a different region of England, and the groups settled in four different regions in America. Each group brought its own culture, what Fischer calls "folkways." While the ethnic composition of regions of our country has changed profoundly over time, it is striking, Fischer argues, how persistent these regional cultures have remained, even over centuries. They, and their regional roots in England, form the basis of the regional cultures we still have in America today.

Puritans from the eastern counties of England constituted the first of the four English migrations; they settled in Massachusetts, and greater New England. The second migration involved "cavaliers and indentured servants" from southern England, who settled in Virginia and the tidewater South. Third, there was the "Friends' migration"— Quakers, from England's North Midlands, who settled in the Delaware Valley (New Jersey, Pennsylvania, Delaware, and northern Maryland). And finally, people from the borderlands—England's northern counties, the Scottish lowlands, and the north of Ireland. They generally settled, Fischer argues, in America's backcountry and southern highlands.

Fischer compares numerous characteristics of each region's culture, not merely different speech and food traditions, but differences having to do with, among other things, family, marriage, childrearing, dress, work, sport, time, death, and inheritance. He explores cultural attitudes about rank—was it hierarchical, egalitarian, or something else? How deferential were people in the different regions to rank and wealth? What were their notions of honor focused on? What were the levels of taxation, voting, literacy, and crime in these different regions? Particularly striking, if you're interested in issues affecting overarching national identity and government, are the regional differences related to freedom, power, order or authority, and wealth. These four waves of English immigration and their different cultures help us understand why states that are in those four different regions are so different from each other today—states like Massachusetts, Virginia, New Jersey, and West Virginia or South Carolina.

My goal here is not to prove Fischer's complex, ambitious, and somewhat controversial thesis, but merely to provide this briefest of summaries of it, because to consider these specific facets of our nation's different regional cultures is to wrestle with the cultural identities and assumptions that underlie the fracture lines in our political landscape today.

Frederick Douglass on the Fourth of July

July 2, 2008

On July 5, 1852, Frederick Douglass, the former slave turned eloquent author and prominent abolitionist, spoke near his home in Rochester, New York at an event commemorating the Declaration of Independence.

Today his powerful words bring to mind contemporary discussions of race in America and attitudes of today's white middle-income voters. They give us much to think about, including the different kinds of patriotism and love of country, and the ongoing process of making "a more perfect union."

Douglass begins his remarks respectfully, calling the signers of the Declaration of Independence brave men, "statesmen, patriots, and heroes... great men, too, great enough to give fame to a great age." Although he acknowledges that "the point from which I am compelled to view them is not, certainly, the most favorable," he honors their memory, noting that he "cannot contemplate their great deeds with less than admiration."

Then, bluntly, Douglass asks why he was asked to speak, and what he, or those still oppressed by slavery whom he represents, have to do with national independence. "This Fourth July," he asserts, "is yours, not mine. You may rejoice, I must mourn. To drag a man in fetters into the grand illuminated temple of liberty, and call upon him to join you in joyous anthems, were inhuman mockery and sacrilegious irony." And he asks, "Do you mean, citizens, to mock me, by asking me to speak today?" Douglass asserts that to a slave, July Fourth is "a day that reveals to him, more than all other days in the year, the gross injustice and cruelty to which he is the constant victim. To him," Douglas continues, "your celebration is a sham; your boasted liberty an unholy license; your national greatness, swelling vanity;... your sermons and thanksgivings... a thin veil to cover up crimes which would disgrace a nation of savages."

Frederick Douglass gave this speech more than ten years before the Emancipation Proclamation. He concludes by saying that, despite the continued existence of slavery, he does not despair of the country because America's history of race is not static and unchanging. There are, he says, "forces in operation which must inevitably work the downfall of slavery." They include the abolitionist movement, but also, he says, "tendencies of the age"—global commerce, a decline in national isolation, the spread of knowledge from the few to the many, and the spread of intelligence across the globe. And so, he says, he concludes where he began, with hope.

Our younger daughter's middle name is Hope. People sometimes ask me whether it's a family name. I say, no, just a good idea. Hope is faith in progress, a conviction that things can change for the better. Hope is not a strategy, but it is essential. For without hope comes despair, and we know from events both at home and abroad, that despairing people—people who believe they have nothing to lose—can do terrible things.

In Fact, It was Slavery

February 1, 2011

It's often said that history is written by the victors. The American Civil War, which has its 150th anniversary between 2011 and 2015, is an exception to that rule. For nearly a century, its history was largely written by Southerners, who asserted, among other things, that the South seceded not to preserve slavery, but on a matter of principle—states' rights. That's what a lot of us were taught growing up. In recent decades, however, most historians agree that the war was, in fact, about slavery.

For example, in February 1861 delegates to a state convention in Texas voted to secede, making Texas the seventh state to do so. If one looks at what they and other states said about why they were seceding, it's one issue—slavery. Yes, they asserted forcefully that states have the right to secede, but the reason they felt compelled to exercise that right was slavery. In Texas they wrote specifically about the North's hostility to what they called the South's "beneficent and patriarchal system of African slavery, [and the North's advocating] the debasing doctrine of the equality of all men, irrespective of race or color—a doctrine at war with nature, in opposition to the experience of mankind, and in violation of the plainest revelations of the Divine Law."

Why has the war's cause been such a sensitive issue? First, after the war, even the South recognized that the preservation of slavery was hardly an idealistic cause. Moreover, after the war, we all—north and south—wanted to move beyond the war and the division. We were reluctant to talk about the ugly truth that race, and slavery, was the nub of the matter, and the inconvenient fact that the North was to some degree complicit with that "peculiar institution." The North's economy, especially manufacturing and banking, was linked to the perpetuation of slavery in the South.

And so, as writer Robert Penn Warren, historian David Blight, and others have pointed out, America implicitly agreed not to talk about slavery; we agreed to let Reconstruction fail in the South. (We do get compassion fatigue sometimes, and weary of nation-building, too.) The nation agreed to let southern blacks be disenfranchised and resubjugated under Jim Crow. Indeed, it might be said that the South lost the war but won the peace. We agreed to honor the bravery, sacrifice, and dedication of those who fought on each side, and, like a dysfunctional family, agreed not to talk about why eleven southern states seceded.

There's a famous photo from the fiftieth anniversary of the Battle of Gettysburg in 1913, of old veterans, white men wearing blue and gray, shaking hands where they had once fought a bloody battle. That reconciliation of North and South may only have been possible because black Americans had been written out of the story.

It would take a century before the Civil Rights movement insisted that we address the issue of race. Even 150 years later, our nation still wrestles with it.

The Supreme Court Justice and the Klan

June 30, 2010

West Virginia Senator Robert Byrd died in 2010 at the age of ninety-two. He was the longest-serving senator in United States history, and it's well known that he was once a member of the Ku Klux Klan. But he was not the only hugely influential person who had been a member of the Klan.

Hugo LaFayette Black represented Alabama in the U.S. Senate from 1927 to 1937. President Franklin Roosevelt then nominated him to the Supreme Court, where he served from 1937 to 1971—not so long ago. He was the fifth longest-serving justice in our history and one of the most influential justices of the twentieth century.

Hugo Black was born in 1886 in a small wooden farmhouse in the hills of Clay County, Alabama, the youngest of eight children. He joined the Klan in 1923, when he was a young trial lawyer in Birmingham. He did so to ingratiate himself with the Klan-dominated juries of the time and to win Klan members' votes when he ran for the Senate. Hugo Black's thirty-five years on the Supreme Court reflected his ongoing effort to rectify that egregious error.

Three years after joining the Court, Black wrote one of his most memorable opinions, *Chambers v. Florida*, which overturned, as a violation of due process of law, the convictions of four poor black tenant farmers who, without counsel and after nine days and nights of relentless police questioning, had confessed to a murder. Former Dean of the University of Pennsylvania Law School and Dartmouth College President Emeritus James O. Freedman wrote that, "In a single, ringing sentence, Justice Black reproached and redeemed his past: 'Under our Constitutional system, [Black wrote,] courts stand against any winds that blow as havens of refuge for those who might otherwise suffer because they are helpless, weak, outnumbered, or because they are non-conforming victims of prejudice and public excitement.'"

Hugo Black had little formal education, and yet over a lifetime of study and reflection, he pursued a course of self-education that, Freedman argued, was probably unprecedented in the Court's history. He read political philosophy and history—from classical authors to the Enlightenment and our Founding Fathers—and in the process he grew, and he evolved a judicial philosophy that was hugely influential on the development of American Constitutional law.

For those reasons, Justice Black was a kind of personal hero for Freedman. At the beginning of one academic year, Freedman held Black up to students as an examplar, because Black represented for him humans' capacity for lifelong growth and development, and because Black transcended his narrow and prejudiced time and place to pursue his own path and to serve a judicial philosophy that was not ideologically but conceptually defined.

Some years ago a president stated, with what I considered tragically misplaced pride, his confidence that the opinions or thinking of his nominee to the Court wouldn't "evolve" over time. From time to time, as the U.S. Senate considers a new nominee to the Supreme Court, we may do well to remember that in the face of experience and reflection both Senator Byrd and Justice Hugo Black changed, they grew, and their thinking evolved. And they and the country were the better for it.

The Honorable John Gilbert Winant

November 15, 2010

John Gilbert Winant was a young Republican progressive who served as governor of New Hampshire from 1925 to 1927 and from 1931 to 1935. After Winant criticized his own party for its vicious attacks on Social Security (which effectively ended his promising future in his party), President Franklin Roosevelt appointed him the first head of the Social Security Board. In 1941, Roosevelt named him ambassador to Great Britain.

Ambassador Winant's predecessor, Joseph Kennedy, thought Britain's defeat by Germany was inevitable and favored appeasement. But Winant was with Britain to his core, and Britain was thrilled at his appointment: "There is something of the knight errant about him," *The Times* wrote. "He believes in his principles with almost romantic passion."

Winant and two other men—Edward R. Murrow, head of CBS News in Europe, and Averell Harriman, head of Roosevelt's Lend-Lease program—are the focus of Lynne Olson's superb book entitled, *Citizens of London: The Americans Who Stood with Britain in Its Darkest, Finest Hour*. With Germany strangling its supply lines across the Atlantic and the Luftwaffe attacking from the air in anticipation of invasion, Great Britain was really on the ropes. Winant and Murrow worked to help Britain get all the support America could provide, even before we entered the war. While Murrow spoke directly to the American people, Winant mediated between a desperate British prime minister and, according to Olson, a politically cautious American president.

Winant and Harriman became part of Churchill's inner circle. Indeed they were with Churchill when news came of the attack on Pearl Harbor. Winant walked the streets of London during the heaviest bombing raids asking how he could help, and his deep caring moved the British people profoundly.

Shy and soft-spoken, Winant was a halting and awkward speaker, but once he got going, he could be incredibly eloquent; he was so full of idealism, sincerity, and compassion that audiences absolutely loved him. When a coal miners' strike threatened British war production and the country's fragile economy, it was the American ambassador, of all people, whom the government asked to go speak with the miners. Speaking from the heart, he persuaded his audience, and the strike ended. One paper compared his speech to the Gettysburg Address, and argued that it should "be committed to memory, recited in all the schools, preached about in all the churches."

In 1944, Roosevelt considered making Winant his running mate. But close advisers didn't share his enthusiasm for the idea, and Roosevelt chose Harry Truman instead. But sixteen months after Roosevelt's death, it was Winant who had the honor of giving the keynote address at FDR's memorial service in the Capitol.

He was brilliant and accomplished, deeply loved and admired. But Winant's inspiring story has a sad ending, because he committed suicide at his home in Concord, New Hampshire in November 1947—on the day that his autobiography was published. Exhausted and depressed, he too, it seems, was a casualty of the war.

Lessons from The Marine's Hymn

April 26, 2005

Protestant minister and author William Sloane Coffin, who lived in Strafford, Vermont, once told me about his experience as a high school senior at Phillips Academy in Andover, Massachusetts. He graduated from Andover, as did his classmate, George Herbert Walker Bush, in 1942, just six months after Pearl Harbor.

Reverend Coffin recalls how his American history teacher, Arthur Burr Darling, made the boys stand up and sing "The Marine's Hymn." Darling ordered Coffin to lead them because Coffin was head of the glee club:

From the Halls of Montezuma,

To the shores of Tripoli,

We fight our country's battles

In the air, on land and sea.

Darling walked to the window, and after a long pause he said, without turning around, "Gentlemen, what were we doing in the halls of Montezuma and in Tripoli?"

Obviously, it made a big impression on young Bill Coffin. The former President Bush has said that Darling was "tough, demanding," and the best teacher he ever had, a teacher who made American "history come alive."

It might be noted that, later in his career, Darling was chosen to write the official history of the CIA's early years. Darling's former student, George H. W. Bush, would later become director of the CIA, and coincidentally, Darling's history would be declassified in 1989, when Bush was president.

But what is the answer to the question Darling asked in class? Why were Americans fighting in the halls of Montezuma and on the shores of Tripoli? The answer is that President Thomas Jefferson had ordered American marines to North Africa without Congressional authorization and despite opposition, even within his own cabinet, to put down the Barbary Coast pirates involved in attacking American and other ships, kidnapping, and ransom. On April 25, 1805 the Marines attacked and captured the key harbor fort at Derna, on "the shores of Tripoli." It was the first time that the American flag had been raised on foreign soil. Alas, it was only America's first military action against Libya.

And what about "the halls of Montezuma"? Those words refer to the climactic battle of the Mexican-American War, 1846-1848. The war ended after General Winfield Scott defeated the Mexicans at the fortified hilltop castle of Chapultepec ("the halls of Montezuma") and then occupied Mexico City.

Many historians argue that the American president, James K. Polk, intentionally provoked war with Mexico to gain territory. Congressman Abraham Lincoln called the war unconstitutional and unnecessary. Whether the war was an intentional land grab or not, it did result in Mexico recognizing the Rio Grande as the boundary of Texas, and the United States acquiring what is now California, Utah, Nevada, most of Arizona, and part of New Mexico, Colorado, and Wyoming.

And so coming together in one story are two phrases in a song, two American presidents—Jefferson and Polk—who intervened to advance American interests as they saw them, and a third American president and his history teacher who sought to learn from history so as not to be doomed to repeat it.

Manzanar and the Lone Ranger

October 16, 2008

O ne summer recently, I went hiking in the high Sierras of California, a mountain range that runs north-south, with the Central Valley on the west and Death Valley on the east. Not only was the hiking spectacular, but in Lone Pine and Independence, the towns where my hike began and ended, I found two new historical, cultural sites that were not far apart. Both related largely to the same period of American history, the 1940s, but they embodied very different aspects of that time.

The first is the Museum of Lone Pine Film History. It turns out that the hills just outside the small California town of Lone Pine were, from the 1920s to the sixties, the setting for over 400 Hollywood movies. Most of them were B-westerns, featuring stars like Gene Autry, Roy Rogers, Tex Ritter, "Gabby" Hayes, William Boyd as Hopalong Cassidy, Randolph Scott, and John Wayne. It was also the setting for the TV show "The Lone Ranger." The movies were virtually mass-produced and highly formulaic: good guys versus bad guys, lots of fistfights, chase scenes, and shootouts. Not too far from Hollywood, the region's striking rock formations and snow-capped Sierras in the background made it an ideal movie location.

With the significant exception of the typical Western's portrayal of Native Americans, those films are looked at as wholesome, moral, all-American entertainment, without sex or graphic violence; they are movies in which the good guys win and the villains are punished. They may not have been great movies, but for many people they embody some of the best American ideals—gritty independence, honesty, the pursuit of justice, and basic decency.

In contrast, the second site I visited was the Manzanar National Historic Site. Run by the National Park Service, Manzanar War Relocation Center was one of ten camps where 110,000 Japanese Americans—men, women, and children living on the west coast—were interned during World War II. Located between Lone Pine and the town of Independence, the camp was opened in 1942; fifty years later, in 1992, the National Historic Site was established. I knew the story of the Japanese internments, but still found the exhibit both informative and deeply moving. I learned, for example, of Pfc. Sadao Munemori, who, a month before the war ended in Europe, died throwing himself on a grenade to save others. He received the Medal of Honor posthumously. At the time, his mother and siblings were interned at Manzanar.

And I was struck by the boldness of one exhibit panel at the National Historic Site. It featured two photographs side by side, one of the U.S.S. Arizona burning after being bombed at Pearl Harbor, the other of smoke pouring from the World Trade Center on 9/11, and beside them the well-known quotation from Benjamin Franklin, saying, "Those who would give up Essential Liberty to purchase a little Temporary Safety, deserve neither Liberty nor Safety."

Two historic sites embodying America's history, neither of them particularly well known, stand in stark contrast and virtually side by side in the high desert country of California, speaking powerfully of America's past and of fundamental American values and ideals.

Eisenhower, Kennedy, and Preventive War

July 13, 2004

hat I read was so chilling, so amazing, that it has stuck with me
for years. In his book *Dark Sun: The Making of the Hydrogen
Bomb*, Pulitzer Prize-winner Richard Rhodes describes how, as early as
the late 1940s, high-level civilian and military strategists seriously considered attacking the Soviet Union—then, before it had nuclear weapons. In 1953, when the Soviets were rapidly building their nuclear capability, retired Air Force General James Doolittle chaired a committee
that recommended that the Soviet Union be given two years to come to
nuclear terms with the U.S., or we would attack. President Eisenhower
quickly rejected this stunning idea.

The issue arose again in spring 1954 when a Joint Chiefs of Staff
study group briefed President Eisenhower on a proposal to "deliberately precipitat[e] war with the USSR ... before the USSR could achieve
a large enough thermonuclear capability to be a real menace to [the]
Continental U.S." However, Army Chief of Staff Matthew Ridgway told
the president he thought the proposal "contrary to every principle
upon which our Nation had been founded...and that...it would be ab-
horrent to the great mass of the American people." Again, Eisenhower
nixed a preventive war.

But that wasn't the end of it. The CIA estimated that the Soviets
would need a month to assemble and deliver all their nuclear weapons.
So General Curtis LeMay, commander of our nuclear-armed bombers—
the Strategic Air Command—and later Air Force Chief of Staff, was
authorized to plan for a preemptive attack if intelligence indicated that
the USSR was beginning a first strike.

LeMay did more than that. He used reconnaissance flights over the
Soviet Union to gather intelligence, knowing—and apparently hop-
ing— that in doing so he might be actually provoking war. He report-

edly told a flight crew, "Maybe if we do this overflight right, we can get World War III started." After retirement, he reiterated that we'd have been a lot better off "if we'd got World War III started in those days."

And incredibly, at the height of the Cuban Missile Crisis, when the world stood on the brink of nuclear war, the Strategic Air Command launched an intercontinental ballistic missile across the Pacific as part of a test that had been scheduled before the crisis and that could easily have been cancelled or rescheduled. Richard Rhodes calls it "a deliberate provocation [of war], unsanctioned, and potentially catastrophic."

There's no question that the Soviets' nuclear capacity grew rapidly during those years; no question that its leadership was utterly ruthless. After all, mass murderer Joseph Stalin only died in March 1953. Those were indeed dangerous times, but few today would agree with General LeMay that we'd have been better off had we intentionally precipitated World War III.

What JFK Would Have Said in Dallas

November 19, 2007

While it is intriguing to speculate on "what might have been" had President Kennedy not been assassinated, doing so is a largely futile exercise. But we do know what he would have said in the speech that he would have given that afternoon in Dallas, and it may reflect some important lessons Kennedy learned as president.

On November 22, 1963, President Kennedy was to speak at the new Graduate Research Center in Dallas. Of course, he never had the chance. Given that setting, his remarks would, appropriately, have dealt with the importance of learning, knowledge, and reason.

Kennedy would have said, "Th[e] link between leadership and learning is not only essential at the community level. It is even more indispensable in world affairs. Ignorance and misinformation can handicap the progress of a city or a company, but they can, if allowed to prevail in foreign policy, handicap this nation's security. In a world of complex and continuing problems ... America's leadership must be guided by the lights of learning and reason or else those who confuse rhetoric with reality and the plausible with the possible will gain the popular ascendancy with their seemingly swift and simple solutions to every world problem."

The speech continued, "[Our nation's] strength will never be used in pursuit of aggressive ambitions—it will always be used in pursuit of peace. It will never be used to promote provocations—it will always be used to promote the peaceful settlement of disputes."

I find these words interesting, especially given that shortly after becoming president, Kennedy had approved the Bay of Pigs invasion of Cuba, which, it turned out, was based on ignorance, misinformation, and confusion between rhetoric and reality—precisely what he would have warned us about in Dallas. Nor was the Bay of Pigs about the peaceful settlement of disputes; it was about the violent overthrow of a foreign government.

Perhaps this speech, never given, suggests that President Kennedy had learned from the Bay of Pigs, realizing that foreign policy needs to be grounded firmly in reality and that as president, he should listen to even experts' advice with a certain skepticism. He had followed their advice about the Bay of Pigs to our detriment; but eighteen months later, during the Cuban Missile Crisis, when his advisors argued that attacking Cuba was the only viable option, he wisely rejected that counsel in favor of a blockade.

Idealistic and religious, Kennedy felt that long-term success requires that our actions be not only grounded in learning, reason, and reality, but also that they be right and just. Had he lived, his speech in Dallas would have concluded with these stirring words:

> We in this country, in this generation, are ... the watchmen on the walls of world freedom. We ask, therefore, that we may be worthy of our power and responsibility, that we may exercise our strength with wisdom and restraint, and that we may achieve in our time and for all time the ancient vision of 'peace on earth, good will toward men.' That must always be our goal, and the righteousness of our cause must always underlie our strength. For as was written long ago: 'Except the Lord keep the city, the watchman waketh but in vain.'

Wall Street's First Terrorist Bombing

August 19, 2011

A terrorist attack in mid September. High casualties. The site: New York City's financial district, the epicenter of global capitalism and banking. No, we're not talking about 9/11, but an event that happened on September 16, 1920.

At noon on that date, a horse-drawn wagon stopped at the intersection of Broad Street and Wall Street. It was called simply "the Corner," and it was the location of J. P. Morgan and Company, the world's most powerful financial institution. On the wagon, a timer was attached to a hundred pounds of dynamite and five hundred pounds of cast iron window sash weights. When the bomb detonated, the window weights became deadly shrapnel. Thirty-eight people died; hundreds were wounded. Until the Oklahoma City bombing in 1995, this was the worst act of terrorism in American history. If you visit Wall Street, look for the pockmarks from the explosion on the white marble building at 23 Wall Street.

Those responsible for the bombing were never found, despite a three-year international investigation that involved the head of the Justice Department's new division that investigated radical groups—a young man named J. Edgar Hoover. Also involved was Attorney General A. Mitchell Palmer, who is remembered now principally as the architect of the Palmer Raids, aggressive efforts to arrest and deport left-wing radicals. Many people were highly critical of Palmer's methods and willingness to short-circuit the legal system and deportation processes.

It was a scary time. The Russian Revolution of 1917 had stirred concerns about anarchists, Bolsheviks, and labor agitators. In the previous year or so, thirty mail bombs had been sent to prominent government officials and businessmen, and bombs had been detonated in numerous American cities.

The Wall Street bombing isn't particularly well known today. But when it happened, it struck fear into the nation. We know now that the sky didn't fall, and neither the country nor capitalism collapsed either; the anarchists or whoever planted the bomb didn't win the day. But of course at the time, people on Wall Street, the government, and American citizens generally didn't know what would happen next.

Today we can be confident that 9/11 won't be forgotten, as the Wall Street Bombing largely has been. What we don't know today is how long the shadow of those terrorist attacks of ten years ago will be. The shadow of the Pearl Harbor attack on December 7th, 1941 was bloody but, in fact, comparatively short. (World War II lasted less than four years, and relations with Japan were normalized not many years later.) The shadow of the American Civil War, on the other hand, has stretched out for more than a century and indeed still lingers in some ways today, 150 years later.

If 9/11 began a new chapter in American or even world history, how long will that chapter be? And what will the world look like when the battle with radical Islam is played out? Only time will tell.

The Power
and Pleasure
of Poetry

RFK's Extemporaneous Eulogy for MLK

April 3, 2008

In early April 1968, Senator Robert F. Kennedy was on the campaign trail for the Democratic nomination for president. When he landed in Indianapolis, a staff member pulled him aside and told him that Reverend Martin Luther King had been shot and killed in Memphis. Senator Kennedy walked straight to the microphone and told the assembled crowd he had "sad news for them and for people who love peace all over the world, and that is that Martin Luther King was shot and killed tonight in Memphis, Tennessee."

With a calming voice and gentle eloquence, Kennedy said that Martin Luther King, Jr. had dedicated his life to love and justice and that he died in the cause of that effort. He said that at this difficult time we might ask ourselves what kind of nation we are and what direction we want to move in. He asked whether we wanted to move toward polarization, bitterness, hatred, and revenge, or whether we want to try, as Martin Luther King did, to replace violence with an effort to understand with compassion and love.

"For those of you who are black and are tempted to be filled with hatred and distrust at the injustice of such an act, against all white people," Kennedy said, " I can only say that I feel in my own heart the same kind of feeling. I had a member of my family killed, but he was killed by a white man. But we have to make an effort in the United States, ... to go beyond these rather difficult times."

Part of the reason that these comments were so powerful was that they were deeply personal and deeply felt. Kennedy said, "My favorite poet was Aeschylus. He once wrote: 'In our sleep, pain which cannot forget falls drop by drop upon the heart until, in our own despair, against our will, comes wisdom through the awful grace of God.'"

Bobby didn't quote Aeschylus because he was a highfalutin intellectual. He did so because after having personally experienced great loss and sorrow, after reading and thinking deeply, these powerful lines that are both painful and healing came to his mind. And so at that excruciating moment, he was able to speak powerfully and authentically when most of us would have been left literally speechless.

Kennedy concluded his speech by saying, "Let us dedicate ourselves to what the Greeks wrote so many years ago: to tame the savageness of man and make gentle the life of the world. Let us dedicate ourselves to that, and say a prayer for our country and our people."

That is the power of poetry and reading, the power of the humanities, and the power of a life of thoughtful reflection. They help us not only remember and speak, but also feel and understand.

The Power and Pleasure of Poetry

April 14, 2008

The American poet William Carlos Williams wrote,
>   It is difficult
> to get the news from poems
>   yet men die miserably every day
>   for lack
> of what is found there.

They are powerful lines, even more powerful if you know that William Carlos Williams was a family physician in Paterson, New Jersey, hardly an affluent town; Williams knew firsthand what people died from every day.

Now, it's important to note that Dr. Williams did not say that people are dying miserably because they weren't reading poetry, which may be a relief to non-poetry readers. What he said was that people are dying miserably every day because their lives lack what can be found in poetry: beauty, soul, meaning, emotion, ideas, powerful connections with important things and everyday things alike. In other words, the stuff that makes us human.

People are often intimidated by poetry; some find it hard to understand. Some have the sense that poems are full of Deep Hidden Meaning—DHM—and our job as readers is to ferret it out. Of course, some poetry is difficult to understand, but much is not.

Many males—particularly boys—consider poetry a female do-main, one that has nothing to say to them. But poetry has much to offer everyone. Sometimes doubting students need to be exposed to poems that rid them of that notion that poetry has cooties, or that poetry is for wimps. They haven't seen poems that really pack a punch, like Randall Jarrell's poem "The Death of the Ball Turret Gunner," or Auden's poem "Funeral Blues," or A.E. Housman's "To an Athlete Dying Young," or Wilfred Owen's poem about World War I, "Dulce et Decorum Est," or Robert Frost's "Out, Out—." When they realize that maybe poems can speak to them, they are open to other poems about other things, even love, beauty, and the power of everyday events.

There are lots of good collections of poetry for people who want to give it a try. Garrison Keillor has edited one, and you can also sign up on the web to get his Writers Almanac poem emailed to you every day. If you don't understand a poem, read it more than once. If you don't like it or still don't understand it, don't worry about it; move on. After all, some paintings in a museum you like more than others, and some paintings, I confess, I don't get at all. The same is true for poems.

I'm pleased to say that poetry is making something of a comeback in this country, thanks to Garrison Keillor, rap music, slam poetry, some innovative projects by national poet laureates, and countless other factors. The key thing, Dr. William Carlos Williams might argue, is that we all somehow, somewhere, find in our lives the power and passion, the beauty and meaning, that can be found in poetry.

The Poetry of Pitching

June 3, 2008

B aseball is not so much a game as it is a mindset, a way of life—even, for some, a religion. The American poet Robert Francis, who lived from 1901 to 1987, wrote a charming poem entitled "The Pitcher." It's about how a pitcher wants to mislead the batter. More accurately, he wants the batter to understand, but only when it's too late. Pitching, the poet says, is an art: it involves technique and passion. Above all, it is subtle and nuanced; the difference between one kind of pitch and another, between a ball and a strike, is ever so slight.

That nuance is suggested in the poet's using two words side by side that are almost identical in meaning and sound: errant and arrant. An errant pitch is one that is wrong, that deviates from the regular course, that wanders. An arrant pitch means the same thing, but it's worse—a really wild pitch. The difference between the two? No more than a slight vowel change.

Here's Robert Francis's "The Pitcher":

His art is eccentricity, his aim
How not to hit the mark he seems to aim at,
His passion how to avoid the obvious,
His technique how to vary the avoidance.

The others throw to be comprehended. He
Throws to be a moment misunderstood.
Yet not too much. Not errant, arrant, wild,
But every seeming aberration willed.

Not to, yet still, still to communicate
Making the batter understand too late.

Now, make no mistake: this is a poem about baseball. But any time you have a poet talking about someone being an artist, you can be pretty sure he's talking about poetry as well. The words he uses relate to poetry at least as much as to baseball: eccentricity, passion, technique, being comprehended, being for a moment misunderstood, communicating, avoiding the obvious, not hitting the mark he seems to aim at.

A poet doesn't want to mislead a reader, like a pitcher wants to mislead a batter. But, as Robert Frost once said, poetry is the one acceptable way to say one thing and mean another. Moreover, like a pitcher, a poet doesn't want to be obvious and hit you over the head with a message, cliché, or symbol. Poets, too, use nuance—the various connotations of words, for example—to hit the mark. And just as pitchers love a change-up, poets want to avoid the clickity-clack of doggerel verse, with its unerring, predictable meter and rhyme. Frost spoke, for example, of liking the straight crookedness of a good walking stick.

This is only to show what every fan of America's pastime already knows: that there is artistry in baseball—even poetry.

Alexander Pope's Satirical Olympic Games

March 8, 2010

In 1743 the distinguished English poet Alexander Pope published a satiric poem entitled "The Dunciad." Pope, like Jonathan Swift (the author of *Gulliver's Travels* and "A Modest Proposal"), was a satirist; his works ridiculed vice and folly, usually lambasting human faults and foolishness in general, but sometimes naming names. It's been said that society licenses satirists to draw blood in service of the health of the body politic. Sometimes they use a scalpel, sometimes a butcher knife.

As a writer, Pope particularly went after those writers, critics, and readers whom he thought were dull, tasteless, stupid, or corrupt. He went after plagiarists, and there were many in an age before copyright. He went after third-rate authors and poets as well as their publishers, patrons, and public. And he did it with great skill and artfulness. In its style, "The Dunciad" parodies Homer, not to ridicule that classical poet, but in part to suggest how far beneath Homer's epic heroes the dunces are whom he satirizes.

"The Dunciad" portrays an upside down world in which quality and excellence are denounced, and the dunces, dullards, and dopes are honored and adored. Indeed the dunces rule, presiding over the demise of all that Pope values: quality, taste, honesty, intelligence. The goddess Dulness chooses as King of Dunces Colley Cibber, a minor-league but highly honored writer of Pope's day. In Cibber's honor she hosts heroic games, an edgy parody of the Olympic games of ancient Greece. To be clear, Pope is not ridiculing heroic games; he's using them as a vehicle to ridicule the vice and folly he sees all around him.

Needless to say, Pope changes the games in his mock epic, making some of them scatological. In one game, critics compete to see who can make the most meaningless noise and impress the king of monkeys. In another, the works of two authors are read aloud to determine which is the dullest, and therefore the best. But everyone keeps falling asleep.

In those days to "tickle with a feather" or quill pen meant to flatter someone, and so there's a tickling contest to see which author can get money from patrons by flattering them the most. Each writer is more obsequious than the previous one. The winner? A man with absolutely no talent who sends his sister to visit the judge.

My favorite event is a sewer diving contest among political hack writers, with prizes for the one who flings the most filth and the one who dives the deepest. I find that contest, crude as it is, particularly appropriate as I think about political hack writers today.

Just as the Olympic games of ancient Greece continue today, the satirists' work also continues: ridiculing vice and folly, which persist in abundance.

Emily Dickinson and Gary Gilmore

June 21, 2005

First it was Terri Schiavo and the controversy surrounding her right to die. Then the papers were full of stories about proposed "death with dignity" legislation. Proponents said the law would provide terminally ill sufferers with end-of-life choices, including "a controlled, prescribed, legal means to obtain their final freedom."

Executions are in the news, too. Connecticut had its first execution in over forty years. And Vermont, which doesn't have capital punishment, had its first capital case in fifty years because the accused was charged with a federal crime for which he could have been put to death.

All this talk of executions and the right to die took me back to a high school English class I taught more than thirty years ago. It was my first year of teaching, and we were studying the poetry of Emily Dickinson, whose life spanned the middle of the nineteenth century. For days, the national news had been full of coverage of the impending execution in Utah of murderer Gary Gilmore, who had refused all efforts to stop his execution: he preferred execution to life in prison. Multiple, frantic efforts were made to save his life. Norman Mailer's book *The Executioner's Song* tells Gilmore's story.

On the morning of January 17th, 1977, Gilmore was strapped to a chair in front of a firing squad of five volunteers. Four of the rifles had bullets; the fifth rifle fired a blank—so that each man might hold out the thought that he did not help kill another human being. Asked if he had any last words, Gilmore replied simply, "Let's do it." And they did.

When I walked into class that morning, I asked the students to turn their poetry books to a certain page, and without any reference to the morning's events, we read a seven-line poem.

The right to perish might be thought
An undisputed right—
Attempt it, and the Universe
Upon the opposite
Will concentrate its officers—
You cannot even die
But nature and mankind must pause
To pay you scrutiny.

The students were stunned. In part, it was the obvious connection between the poem and Gilmore's death. But it was also the revelation that a poem could pack such a whollop—especially a poem by such a fragile, reclusive nineteenth century woman who, to their minds, was so removed and protected from the rough and tough real world.

Some of the students had had a sense that poetry had little or nothing to say to them and, certainly, no ability to move them. It's too bad that so many Americans, particularly men, think that poetry is difficult to understand and irrelevant to their lives. Other poems by Dickinson pack a similar punch, and lots by other poets, too.

The Lonesome Death of William Zantzinger

February 19, 2009

I knew the name William Zantzinger from Bob Dylan's haunting ballad "The Lonesome Death of Hattie Carroll." Frankly, I had assumed the man (whom Dylan calls Zanzinger) was either fictional or had lived long ago, but then in 2009 I learned of his death at the age of sixty-nine. The song's first three lines outline the facts. And as literary critic Christopher Ricks points out, the lyrics sound like "a newspaper item with a cadence."

> William Zanzinger (sic) killed poor Hattie Carroll
> With a cane that he twirled around his diamond ring finger
> At a Baltimore hotel society gath'rin'

The murder took place on February 9, 1963. Zantzinger was twenty-four, wealthy, racist, and drunk. Hattie Carroll was fifty-one, a bar maid, and mother of eleven children. She was one of three hotel employees that Zantzinger assaulted that night.

Dylan's ballad has four stanzas; the first three end with this refrain:

> But you who philosophize disgrace and criticize all fears
> Take the rag away from your face
> Now ain't the time for your tears

In the final stanza—and in real life—Zantzinger received a six-month sentence. That's when the refrain changes:

> Bury the rag deep in your face
> For now's the time for your tears

As Ricks points out, "There can be no grosser injustices than those perpetrated by the law itself." Indeed the judges deferred the start of Zantzinger's jail sentence to give him time to harvest his tobacco crop.

Ricks calls this song one of Dylan's greatest, pointing to its excruciating sadness, its "curbed indignation," and the way it avoids melodrama and sentimentality. He points specifically to Dylan's subtle use of rhyme and meter. Nowhere in the song does it say he was white and she was black. That is simply understood.

There's one line in the song that hints that Zantzinger is also, in some way, a victim. It says that he is "Doomed and determined to destroy all the gentle." Yes, the word "determined" conveys his malicious intent, his willfulness in destroying a poor woman who, as the song says elsewhere, "never did nothing to William Zanzinger." That word "doomed," that Zantsinger is somehow doomed himself—brings to my mind something Rev. Martin Luther King Jr. said at Dartmouth College in May 1962, about the pernicious effect that racism and segregation have on whites as well as blacks and the redemptive power of justice and love. He said, "Our victory shall be a double victory. We shall win our opponents in the process."

This song appeared on Dylan's 1964 album *The Times They are A-Changin'*. If these days we needed more proof that times have changed, surely today William Zantsinger would receive more than just a six-month sentence.

Sand Castles and 9/11

January 24, 2005

A year or so after 9/11, I was going through a stack of papers and magazines that I hadn't ever gotten around to reading. In the stack, I confess, was an old *New Yorker* magazine. (I know I'm not the only person who doesn't always read them the week they arrive.) And I was dumbstruck by the magazine's cover. The playful drawing shows three people on the beach building exact replicas of New York City buildings out of sand. She's working on the top of the Chrysler Building, he's sculpting, perhaps, the Citibank building. And there's the top of the Empire State Building, and the twin towers of the World Trade Center. All made of sand.

I was stunned. And then I noticed the date of the magazine: August 6, 2001—just five weeks before September 11th.

I thought of the poem "Ozymandias" by the English poet Percy Bysshe Shelley. It's a poem about how the great manmade monuments (that in our pride look so indestructible) inevitably crumble. Even the massive Bamiyan buddha carved into a cliff in Afghanistan survived 1500 years only to be dynamited into rubble by the ideology, ignorance, intolerance and insecurity of the Taliban.

Here's Shelley's sonnet "Ozymandias":

I met a traveler from an antique land
Who said: "Two vast and trunkless legs of stone
Stand in the desert ... Near them, on the sand,
Half sunk, a shattered visage lies, whose frown
And wrinkled lip, and sneer of cold command,
Tell that its sculptor well those passions read,
Which yet survive, stamped on these lifeless things,
The hand that mocked them, and the heart that fed,

And on the pedestal these words appear:
'My name is Ozymandias, king of kings:
Look upon my works, ye Mighty, and despair!'
Nothing beside remains. Round the decay
Of that colossal wreck, boundless and bare
The lone and level sands stretch far away."

I thought of the countless statues of Saddam Hussein lying discarded in Iraqi junk heaps. And I thought of the Shakespeare sonnet that begins:

Not marble, nor the gilded monuments
Of princes, shall outlive this powerful rhyme...

He may have been right: while statues and buildings rise and fall, here we are, reading his poem four centuries later.

The devastation caused by the Indonesian tsunami the day after Christmas in 2004 made a friend of ours think of the sand castles her kids used to build at the beach when they were young. She said they "always built in the face of disaster," but seldom stayed at the beach long enough to actually see the waves wash the castles away.

In the videos of the Twin Towers crashing to the ground and the tsunami crashing ashore, we saw it happen—humanity and its works destroyed in an instant and not in the slow, inevitable creep of time.

Pray that the Road is Long

June 11, 2008

Students often graduate from high school or college with new goals—things they want to achieve as they "commence" the next chapter in their lives. We set short-term goals, and we set long-term goals having to do perhaps with accomplishing something important, doing good work, or gaining fame or fortune.

The problem is, what then? What do we do when we achieve our goals, when we meet with the success that we've sought for so long? Do we ask, "What now?" "Is that all there is?" To put it another way, what would the dog do if it ever actually caught the car it chased so passionately? Life is about the journey, not the end. We forget that, as Matthew Arnold wrote, "Life is not in having and getting, but in being and becoming." It's so easy to forget that life is what we are doing now.

Life doesn't start some place down the road, after we're "all set," whatever that means. Is it only then, when we are all set (an ever elusive goal if there ever was one), that we begin to enjoy the journey itself, to focus on the present, to begin to act the way we know we should, to start giving back or sharing with others?

One of my favorite poems is entitled "Ithaca," by the great modern Greek poet Constantine Cavafy. In Homer's *Odyssey*, the hero, Odysseus, spends ten years trying to get back home to Ithaca after fighting at Troy. But things keep blowing him off course, delaying his return. Ithaca was his desired destination, but Cavafy's poem surprises us by celebrating the journey itself. Cavafy writes,

> When you set out on your journey to Ithaca,
>   pray that the road is long,
> full of adventure, full of knowledge.

He concludes his poem this way:

Always keep Ithaca in your mind.
To arrive there is your ultimate goal.
But do not hurry the voyage at all.
It is better to let it last for many years;
and to anchor at the isle when you are old,
rich with all you have gained on the way,
not expecting that Ithaca will offer you riches.

Ithaca has given you the beautiful voyage.
Without her you would have never set out on the road.
She has nothing more to give you.

And if you find her poor, Ithaca has not deceived you.
Wise as you have become, with so much experience,
you must already have understood what Ithacas mean.

So that's the challenge—to set and pursue goals, but not mistake
the end for the be-all and end-all. To do that would be to risk approaching the end of one's life, even a successful life, only to realize, to one's
sorrow, that one didn't pay enough attention to the journey or its
meaning.

Blackberry Haiku

December 11, 2006

A midst a recent exchange of wordy, rambling email messages, I got one that was short, crisp, almost telegraphic in its brevity. Then, at the end of the message, I saw the explanation: It said, "Sent from my Blackberry."

I thought of that old comment attributed (like so many other great lines) to Mark Twain: "I didn't have time to write you a short letter, so I wrote you a long one." And I wondered whether this amazing new technology, which I myself have not embraced, might give rise to a new poetic form called Blackberry haiku.

I emailed friends and colleagues, and within a very short time, I had a number of promising haiku, Japanese lyric poems of seventeen syllables in three lines—five syllables, seven syllables, and five syllables. Typically, haiku are imagist poems: they capture sharply and succinctly a single natural image.

The first submission, unsolicited, came from Dean, a novelist in Wisconsin. He wrote:

> My Blackberry buzzed
> and when I threw it, it broke.
> I'm lost. Next time, call.

I thought about how tiny those keyboards are and how difficult it is to type on them. And, with more than a nod to a lovely poem by e e cummings, I offered this:

> You make key strokes count
> With hands smaller than the rain.
> Blackberry haiku.

Brian, a recently retired businessman, also wrote about the small keyboards:

No Blackberry for
me. My two old, obese thumbs
Wreck the lilting prose.

Charlie wrote about big thumbs as well, but with a witty, contemporary allusion to hidden weapons of mass destruction and war—in this case, thumb wars, as we use both thumbs to surreptitiously send messages to friends when we should be paying attention in meetings:

Blackberry's are made
Only for mass distraction;
Hidden thumb parties.

Then Charlie's wife, who'd been copied on all the back and forth, noted with a laugh, how blackberry haiku had caused businessmen to turn to writing poetry:

Makes you wonder. Big
Execs with tiny poets
Trying to get out.

Poetry, like any action, produces an equal and opposite reaction. Sean, in New Hampshire, doesn't have a Blackberry and he doesn't want one for Christmas. He writes,

No Blackberry gift.
Thought, quiet are better things
Than buzz, email, yack.

And Jan, from North Dakota, had the final word, which seems to resonate here in Vermont:

My Blackberry is
purple, luscious, cool, and sweet.
It never buzzes.

4

Robert Frost

The Most Misunderstood Poem in America

October 6, 2011

"The Road Not Taken" is one of Robert Frost's most famous and most beloved poems. It also may be the most misunderstood poem in America.

You see the poem, especially its last stanza, on posters and note cards inspiring us to take the road less traveled by, because doing so will make "all the difference." But is that what the poem really means— that we should march to a different drummer, and go in our own direction? With Frost, things are seldom as simple as they initially appear.

Notice that the title of the poem is not "The Road Less Traveled." A poem with that title might be about marching to a different drummer. Rather, it's entitled, "The Road Not Taken." The title points not to the road he took, but to the road he didn't take.

> Two roads diverged in a yellow wood,
> And sorry I could not travel both
> And be one traveler, long I stood
> And looked down one as far as I could
> To where it bent in the undergrowth;
>
> Then took the other, as just as fair,
> And having perhaps the better claim,
> Because it was grassy and wanted wear;
> Though as for that, the passing there
> Had worn them really about the same.

Notice that the narrator says that one was "just as fair" as the other. Moreover, he immediately revises his assertion that he took one path "Because it was grassy and wanted wear," acknowledging, "Though as for that the passing there/Had worn them really about the same."

Then he continues,

> And both that morning equally lay
> In leaves no step had trodden black.

The two roads were equally worn. In fact, no one had trod either path. How then could one of them be less traveled if no one had set foot on either one?

Sometimes, after we have made a choice, we justify or rationalize our decision by telling ourselves all sorts of good reasons why we did what we did when, in fact, it was more a function of six of one, a half dozen of the other. Rather than acknowledge that to ourselves, we consciously or unconsciously project on to the memory of the decision all sorts of factors that weren't part of the decision at all.

The poem's first three stanzas are written in the past tense. It says, for example, "long I stood/And looked down one..." But importantly, the famous fourth and final stanza is in the future tense. He's making a prediction or an assertion about what he will say many years in the future:

> I shall be telling this with a sigh
> Somewhere ages and ages hence:
> Two roads diverged in a wood, and I—
> I took the one less traveled by,
> And that has made all the difference.

Notice that the narrator is not, in fact, asserting that he took the road less traveled by; he is predicting that years later, he will say that he did, and that that choice had made all the difference. But given the first three stanzas—given what he's told us about what really happened—did he, in fact, choose the road less traveled?

And with what kind of sigh does he envision telling the story of his decision, the story of his life's choices, years from now? It's not entirely clear whether it is a sigh of well-deserved satisfaction that comes from having made sense of how one's life played itself out. Or is it a sigh caused by the narrator predicting that he will recall his decision with positive feelings of self-congratulations even though he knows now that those feelings will, in fact, be the product of revisionist thinking and self-delusion?

After all, our memories of not only what we do but why we do it morphs over time, and while we may be satisfied with the life we've had, we can never know for sure what might have been had we chosen the other path, chosen the "the road not taken."

Celebrating the Present

April 6, 2007

Too often we have difficulty simply being in the present. In his poem "A Prayer in Spring," Robert Frost asks that he recognize the stunning beauty of spring and take pleasure in the present moment. He asks that he not think about the uncertain future harvest, as farmers invariably do—whether it'll be a good one or bad. He wants simply to take pleasure in the beauty of the moment.

Flowers abound, bees buzz, a hummingbird "thrusts in with needle bill." The apple orchard, with its white blossoms, looks, he says, "Like nothing else by day, like ghosts by night." Isn't that a beautiful line? By day, the orchard in bloom has a beauty all its own; in the dark of night, the trees look like ghosts. It makes me think of a painting by Marc Chagall—dark blue and dreamlike.

Frost wrote the poem when he was a young man, perhaps thirty-two. As the title suggests, there's a spiritual—but not necessarily strictly Christian—side to the exuberance the poet feels at the beauty of spring. There's also a sensual side: the thrill he feels at nature's beauty unites with the love he feels for his beloved. Frost's wife, Elinor, is not far beneath the surface of many Frost poems, including this one.

It is the last of the poem's four stanzas that is hardest to understand, particularly just hearing it once. My advice? Read it more than once. If that doesn't help, don't worry about it. For the moment at least, enjoy the rest of the poem.

Here's the poem:

Oh, give us pleasure in the flowers today;
And give us not to think so far away
As the uncertain harvest; keep us here
All simply in the springing of the year.

Oh, give us pleasure in the orchard white,
Like nothing else by day, like ghosts by night;
And make us happy in the happy bees,
The swarm dilating round the perfect trees.

And make us happy in the darting bird
That suddenly above the bees is heard,
The meteor that thrusts in with needle bill,
And off a blossom in mid-air stands still.

For this is love and nothing else is love,
The which it is reserved for God above
To sanctify to what far ends He will,
But which it only needs that we fulfill.

When Frost writes in that last complex stanza, "For this is love and nothing else is love," he's referring to that love that comes from taking pleasure in nature's beauty, from participating joyfully in the springing of the year, and from the renewal of body and spirit that comes from that sanctified beauty. But what is Frost to do with this powerful feeling? Frost asserts that it falls to God to direct that love toward some purpose, and it falls to us to fulfill that purpose. And so "A Prayer in Spring" is both a prayer and a love poem. It expresses a desire to be keenly aware of spring's staggering beauty, to take pleasure in the present moment, and to leave the uncertain future to the future.

A World Torn Loose

September 13, 2011

The terrible flood damage in Vermont caused by Tropical Storm Irene in 2011 brought to mind a poem by Robert Frost that was inspired by an incident Frost witnessed during the great flood of 1927.

In November 1927, Frost was crossing the country by train to attend the inauguration of a new president of Amherst College in Massachusetts on November 4. He never got there, due to the horrific rain that clobbered much of the Northeast that very day and decimated Vermont, killing eighty-four people, including the lieutenant governor.

Looking out of the train window, Frost saw a washed-out bridge and beside it, a car that kept backing up a little each time a bit more earth would fall away from the lip of the precipice. Years later, that image—the collapsing slope of dirt and the car backing up—inspired a poem. It is entitled "One Step Backward Taken." In it, the narrator watches as heavy rains cause a steep slope of earth and rock to collapse, eroding deep into the hillside. The narrator is standing on top of the slope, and only by stepping back just in time does he save himself, as he says, "from going," too.

Here's the poem:

Not only sands and gravels
Were once more on their travels,
But gulping muddy gallons
Great boulders off their balance
Bumped heads together dully
And started down the gully.
Whole capes caked off in slices.
I felt my standpoint shaken
In the universal crisis.

But with one step backward taken
I saved myself from going.
A world torn loose went by me.
Then the rain stopped and the blowing,
And the sun came out to dry me.

Yes, the poem ends with the rain stopping and the sun coming out to dry him. But those who want an unambiguous happy-ever-after ending will have to look elsewhere because in this deeply philosophical poem, the narrator, who may or may not be exactly Frost himself, describes "a world torn loose," where things are "off their balance." Nature is described as thoughtless and uncaring: "great boulders," it says, bump "heads together dully." And this isn't a one-time event. Water often moves sand and gravel; as the poem tells us, "sands and gravels/ Were once more on their travels." The speaker saves himself only by stepping backward, by retreating.

As a result of his experience, the narrator says, "I felt my standpoint shaken/In the universal crisis." He's not just talking about his literal "standpoint," the place he was standing, which obviously changes. Somehow, his perspective is shaken; for him this eroding hillside stands for a "universal crisis." Exactly what the crisis is and how his perspective changes are unclear. The poem was written in late 1945; perhaps it's his perspective on World War II that changes, or his perspective on war itself, or perhaps he simply feels his life to be more precarious than he did before.

Certainly that is a feeling we all have known at some point, some more recently than others.

Fireflies

July 13, 2005

Of all the memories of growing up in the country, I'd wager that catching fireflies—or, as we called them, lightning bugs—ranks second only to taking a plunge in the local swimming hole.

There's the joy of staying up late. In the summer it doesn't even begin to get dark until after 8:30, and so catching fireflies means staying up well after bedtime. There is the joyful abandon of running around in the dark, getting hot and sweaty. There's the camaraderie of doing so with siblings, cousins, and friends.

There's the joy of the chase. Catching the little black beetles is tricky because their on-and-off light makes it a hide-and-seek challenge to cup one's hands carefully around them as they fly, silent and almost invisible, through the darkness. And there's the problem of perspective: the fact that a bug is just a single dot in the dark makes it hard to determine just how close or far away it is.

Scientists can explain the chemical reaction that produces the light, but they don't know how the beetles turn it on and off. Energy conservation enthusiasts would note with admiration that virtually all the energy produced by a firefly is given off as light, not heat. Lightning bugs don't feel warm in your cupped hand as a light bulb would; a light bulb converts only about 10 percent of its energy to light and the rest is wasted as heat.

But for kids, the greatest joy comes from the beetle's apparently miraculous ability to glow. They are literally luminous beings. Many a weary child has fallen asleep watching them with wonder as they glow in a glass jar beside the bed, only to have mom or dad steal in to set the fireflies free again after the child has fallen asleep.

Robert Frost wrote a six-line poem entitled "Fireflies in the Garden." Here it is:

Here come real stars to fill up the upper skies,
And here on earth come emulating flies
That, though they never equal stars in size
(And they were never really stars at heart),
Achieve at times a very starlike start.
Only, of course, they can't sustain the part.

Once, when reciting the poem on a college campus, Robert Frost himself remarked that poems "are fireflies. They represent our lucid intervals and glow only for a moment."

Perhaps, even as children, we have a sense of the transient nature of things. Our fleeting insights, nature, and life itself are always changing. On, off. On, off in the darkness. Catch it if you can; grab it before the light goes out again and it flies away! That's where the challenge is, and the joy.

Poetic Rivalry

July 15, 2008

I was reading a poem by Robert Frost not long ago, and for the first time, I heard in it an echo of one of T.S. Eliot's most famous poems, "The Love Song of J. Alfred Prufrock." Here's the first stanza of Eliot's Prufrock poem. Listen particularly for the last two lines, "Oh, do not ask, 'What is it?'/Let us go and make our visit."

> Let us go then, you and I,
> When the evening is spread out against the sky
> Like a patient etherized upon a table;
> Let us go, through certain half-deserted streets,
> The muttering retreats
> Of restless nights in one-night cheap hotels
> And sawdust restaurants with oyster-shells:
> Streets that follow like a tedious argument
> Of insidious intent
> To lead you to an overwhelming question . . .
> Oh, do not ask, "What is it?"
> Let us go and make our visit.

Eliot's poem was published in the June 1915 edition of *Poetry: A Magazine of Verse*. It really started Eliot's career. The American poet Ezra Pound had urged the magazine's founder to publish Eliot's poetry. Pound was the magazine's man in London, where Frost met him. Just two years earlier, Pound had favorably reviewed Frost's first book in the magazine, helping to launch Frost's career as well as Eliot's. And so, Frost would have kept a keen eye on *Poetry* magazine. Frost scholar Mark Richardson tells me that if Frost hadn't seen Eliot's poem earlier, he most likely would have seen it in September 1915 when he traveled from his home in Franconia, New Hampshire to New York City on literary business.

Here's Frost's poem "A Time to Talk," written either in 1915 or early 1916—right after Eliot's poem was published.

When a friend calls to me from the road
And slows his horse to a meaning walk,
I don't stand still and look around
On all the hills I haven't hoed,
And shout from where I am, "What is it?"
No, not as there is time to talk.
I thrust my hoe in the mellow ground,
Blade-end up and five feet tall,
And plod: I go up to the stone wall
For a friendly visit.

I find it hard to imagine that Frost would have been able to write a poem that concludes, in short, "I don't... shout... What is it? ...I go/For a friendly visit" and do so wholly innocent of the echo with Eliot's memorable lines, "Oh, do not ask, 'What is it?'/Let us go and make our visit."

Did Frost do so with a wink and a grin? I can't help but wonder whether the well-adjusted, sociable, hearty farmer in Frost's poem is using his hoe to make a little dig at that Anglophile Eliot, with his earnest, effete Prufrock, so neurotic and self-conscious. We can't know for certain, but perhaps very early on, Frost set forth here the contrast in style and temperament between Eliot and himself, two literary titans destined to be poetic rivals.

Silken Tents

June 22, 2010

You'll see them as you drive around Vermont in summer—crisp white tents set up in a field or on a lawn, gleaming in the sun. They may have one or more center poles pushing up taut from below. The rented white folding chairs and perhaps caterers' trucks confirm that all this activity is for a wedding and not something more prosaic, like an auction or big tent sale of overstock inventory. No, gleaming white tents and celebrations of love—they seem to go together.

One of the most exquisitely beautiful poems that Robert Frost ever wrote is called "The Silken Tent." And I think of it when I see one of those white wedding tents out in the middle of a field, even though they're canvas and not silk. Middlebury College English professor and Frost biographer Jay Parini considers "The Silken Tent" one of the finest sonnets written in English in the twentieth century. No question about it.

Normally, readers of the poem don't notice that the poem is one long sentence, but they may feel it—how the poem is "of a piece." That's appropriate to the poem's meaning. The poem is also one extended metaphor, or conceit. The narrator describes how the woman he loves is like a silken tent. He describes how the guy-lines that hold the tent all the way around are real but almost unfelt, except when a little breeze pulls one rope slightly taut for a moment, and on the opposite side the ropes go a little slack. Just as in the bonds of a perfect marriage, there is subtle—often unconscious—give and take.

Here's the poem:

She is as in a field a silken tent
At midday when a sunny summer breeze
Has dried the dew and all its ropes relent,

So that in guys it gently sways at ease,
And its supporting central cedar pole,
That is its pinnacle to heavenward
And signifies the sureness of the soul,
Seems to owe naught to any single cord,
But strictly held by none, is loosely bound
By countless silken ties of love and thought
To everything on earth the compass round,
And only by one's going slightly taut
In the capriciousness of summer air
Is of the slightest bondage made aware.

My hope for all newlyweds this summer—indeed, all couples—is for them to be, as Frost writes, "loosely bound by countless silken ties of love and thought," not only between themselves, but, as he writes, "to everything on earth the compass round."

Letting Go of Good Things

October 26, 2004

It's said that Vermont has six seasons: the usual four and mud season, between winter and spring, and stick season between fall and winter, when the leaves are mostly down and trees stand bare under skies that are more often gray than blue. For many, stick season brings with it a sense of loss; we cling to memories of bluer, greener days before the frost was on the pumpkin.

Robert Frost wrote powerfully about that longing in his poem "Reluctance." But "Reluctance" is not just about seasons changing. It's about that reasonable tendency humans have to accept the inevitable passing of good things. But to do that, Frost writes, "to go with the drift of things," would betray the human heart. He argues that one should be reluctant to accept the end of things, even things we know must end.

In a similar spirit, another poet, Dylan Thomas, urged us to "not go gentle into that good night" but to "Rage, rage against the dying of the light." Not that we can keep death at bay, of course, but we don't have to be resigned to it in a way that negates the affirming power of life.

After an evocative description of New England in autumn, the last stanza of "Reluctance" contains the zinger. Frost waits until the last line—almost the very last word—to make it clear that he is talking at least in part about, of all things, love.

Here's Frost's poem:

Out through the fields and the woods
  And over the walls I have wended;
I have climbed the hills of view
  And looked at the world and descended;
I have come by the highway home,
  And lo, it is ended.

The leaves are all dead on the ground,
  Save those that the oak is keeping
To ravel them one by one
  And let them go scraping and creeping
Out over the crusted snow,
  When others are sleeping.

And the dead leaves lie huddled and still,
  No longer blown hither and thither;
The last lone aster is gone;
  The flowers of the witch hazel wither;
The heart is still aching to seek,
  But the feet question "Whither?"

Ah, when to the heart of man
  Was it ever less than a treason
To go with the drift of things,
  To yield with a grace to reason,
And bow and accept the end
  Of a love or a season?

Frost wrote this poem as a young man of twenty, when he thought he had lost the love of his fiancé and future wife, Elinor. There's a melancholy aspect to the poem, but it's also got spunk; it pushes back. I've read this poem at a funeral—because while it's necessary to accept that all things do end, doing so isn't easy, and indeed, one really wouldn't want it to be. Like all great literature, this poem continues to resonate in my mind and helps me cope with whatever endings that life inevitably brings.

Keep Cold

January 8, 2008

Typically, gardeners worry that bitter cold will winter-kill their plants, but a poem by Robert Frost plays with the opposite notion—the counterintuitive fact that for fruit trees in New England, unseasonable warmth can pose as a great a risk as bitter cold. Frost moved from Franconia, New Hampshire to South Shaftsbury, Vermont in 1920 in part, he said, because he wanted a better place to farm, especially to grow apples. He felt that winters in Franconia were too unstable for apple trees. That fall he wrote a friend, "[I] have moved to a stone cottage on a hill at South Shaftsbury in southern Vermont on the New York side near the historic town of Bennington where if I have any money left after repairing the roof in the spring I mean to plant a new Garden of Eden with a thousand apple trees of some unforbidden variety."

Frost's concern for his apple trees in Franconia resulted in his poem, "Good-by and Keep Cold"—probably written in 1919, the year before he moved. The poem's narrator says goodbye to his orchard for the winter, expressing his hope that it will stay cold, free from a warm spell that would cause the trees to bud out too early. The poet writes,

> I don't want it stirred by the heat of the sun.
> (We made it secure against being, I hope,
> By setting it out on a northerly slope.)
> No orchard's the worse for the wintriest storm;
> But one thing about it, it mustn't get warm.
> "... Dread fifty above more than fifty below."

Frost sent a copy of the poem to a friend in Amherst to confirm that the botanical facts were correct. The friend sent the letter on to the chairman of the pomology department at the Massachusetts Agricultural College, who replied that while the fruit facts were accurate, the metrical treatment of some of the lines was faulty, and that he had therefore taken the liberty of improving upon them. Rather than being angry, Frost found the story amusing, and often told the story before saying the poem in public.

Frost's old house in Shaftsbury is now the Robert Frost Stone House Museum. The museum has taken cuttings from surviving old apple trees on the property, and established a small orchard of the five apple varieties that Frost planted with his son. People nationwide can now order their own apple trees descended from Frost's originals. That is, if the new orchard survives the increasing temperature fluctuations of our traditionally cold, but now warming winters.

To a Young Wretch at Christmas Time

December 20, 2006

In one underappreciated Robert Frost poem, the narrator struggles to feel the holiday spirit toward a neighbor who's cut a Christmas tree on his land without asking. The poem is called "To a Young Wretch," and to my mind, the title alone is reason enough to love it. Frost used the poem for his Christmas card in 1937. In the poem the narrator tells how a young man chopped down a spruce tree from the narrator's woods, and dragged it home to use as a Christmas tree. The narrator, who, of course, may or may not be Frost himself, says that he "could have bought [him] just as good a tree." But he acknowledges that being given a tree isn't the same thing as swiping it. I notice that the narrator does not claim that if the boy only asked, he would have given him the tree. And would we have believed him if he had made that assertion of charity?

The narrator summarizes the conflict saying, "It is your Christmases against my woods." Even here, when their interests are diametrically opposed, he argues that it should be thought of not as a conflict between good and evil, but rather as a conflict between two competing goods. He asserts that it becomes easier to understand how God might be thought of as always fighting on both sides of a war at once, if you think of a war as being about competing goods, rather than as a battle between good and evil.

Here's Frost's poem "To a Young Wretch":

As gay for you to take your father's ax
As take his gun – rod – to go hunting – fishing.
You nick my spruce until its fiber cracks,
It gives up standing straight and goes down swishing.
You link an arm in its arm and you lean

Across the light snow homeward smelling green.

I could have bought you just as good a tree
To frizzle resin in a candle flame,
And what a saving 'twould have meant to me.
But tree by charity is not the same
As tree by enterprise and expedition.
I must not spoil your Christmas with contrition.

It is your Christmases against my woods.
But even where, thus, opposing interests kill,
They are to be thought of as opposing goods
Oftener than as conflicting good and evil;
Which makes the war god seem no special dunce
For always fighting on both sides at once.

And though in tinsel chain and popcorn rope
My tree, a captive in your window bay,
Has lost its footing on my mountain slope
And lost the stars of heaven, may, oh, may
The symbol star it lifts against your ceiling
Help me accept its fate with Christmas feeling.

That says it all, doesn't it—the challenge to feel the holiday spirit towards everyone, even someone who has wronged you, who has taken something of yours? Isn't that the challenge all year long—to love your enemy, to love your neighbor as yourself, even if your neighbor is a young wretch?

The Faces of Vermont

July 10, 2003

We went to our friend Julia's fortieth birthday party. They rented the town hall and had a square dance and sing-along. It was a typical Vermont celebration of family and friends, love and belonging. But the evening also reflected a changing Vermont. Julia is Korean American. Her parents came to this country a half-century ago. My wife is Chinese American, her family having emigrated to Hawaii four generations ago. Julia's husband is Caucasian, like me. Their three kids look a bit like each of them, just as our two girls are what they call in Hawaii "hapa"—meaning "half."

During a toast, Julia's father mentioned that he had to do a little extra to succeed in America because he is Asian, and that he taught their children that they might have to do the same. He recalled how twenty years ago, Julia's brother Joe couldn't take a girl to the prom because the girl's father thought Joe didn't have the right skin color, and how another of his children had been complimented in college for speaking without an accent. Nevertheless, Julia's father emphasized, "We are all proud of being American."

Robert Frost spoke about ethnic change in Vermont in a 1923 interview. He said people think of him as a quintessential Yankee, but, he pointed out, his mother was a Scottish immigrant. Frost said,

> I had an aunt in New England who used to talk long and loud about the foreigners who were taking over this country. Across the way from her house stood a French Catholic church which the new people of the village had put up. Every Sunday my aunt would stand at her window, behind the curtain, and watch the steady stream of men and women pouring into church ... She would say, 'My soul!' Just that: 'My soul!'
>
> All the disapproval and indignation and disgust were

concentrated in these two words ... it did strike me very funny for her to be calling upon her soul for help when this mass of industrious people were going to church to save theirs.

Frost continued,

> New England is constantly going through periods of change. In Vermont ... first came the Irish, then the French, and now the Poles. There are those among us who raise their hands in horror at this, but what does it matter? All these people are becoming, have become, Americans.

Ninety years after Frost's interview, more people see such demographic developments as par for the course. The face of Vermont continues to change. Barre, where Scottish granite workers erected a statue of Robert Burns and another statue honors the Italian-American workers who came later, is still home to new Americans from Asia and elsewhere. Like Barre's residents, each person at Julia's party is every bit an American. Their love, generosity of spirit, and American idealism help make this nation great, help us sing the same tune, and help "crown thy good with brotherhood, from sea to shining sea."

5

Vermont, These Green Hills and Silver Waters

Huxley, Wordsworth, and Vermont

September 29, 2008

Although we're comparatively safe from hurricanes up here in Vermont, flooding from Tropical Storm Irene and news each year of deadly tropical storms in the Gulf of Mexico and the Caribbean remind me that the largely peaceful nature we see around us is just one facet of the natural world. Here in beautiful Vermont, the cozy comfort of "these green hills and silver waters" (as our state song calls them) can lull us into believing that this is all there is to nature. But hurricane season reminds us each year that nature can be as terrible as it can be kind. It can inspire awe, fear, and dread, as well as peacefulness and love.

The author Aldous Huxley wrote an essay in 1929 that touches on similar realizations entitled "Wordsworth in the Tropics." It's about the English poet William Wordsworth, who lived in the late 1700s and early 1800s amidst the pastoral hills and silver waters of northern England's beautiful Lake District. He was a Romantic poet, a nature poet who found in the peaceful landscape around him manifestations of the Romantic ideas of harmony, unity, and serenity. Huxley asserts that Wordsworth mistook the pastoral for the natural, forgetting that the sheep and countless miles of stone walls rolling over hill and dale are not nature, but nature tamed, nature recreated in man's own image.

Huxley argues that it's too bad Wordsworth never left Europe. "A voyage through the tropics," he writes, "would have cured him of his too easy and comfortable pantheism. A few months in the jungle would have convinced him that the diversity and utter strangeness of Nature are at least as real and significant as its intellectually discovered unity." Huxley asserts that time in the tropics would have caused Wordsworth to love nature where love was the appropriate emotion, but also, in the face of nature's sinister, hostile, and terrifying aspect, to respect it and fear it.

I love the outdoors, the natural world, and the beauty of Vermont; and I've loved Wordsworth's poetry since I first read it in college. But I love the wild outdoors as well as the domesticated beauty of the Lake District and the Lake Champlain Valley. As a traveler, and former technical mountaineer and dogsledder, I'm drawn also to the awful starkness of African deserts and the Barren Lands of the subarctic, the unforgiving power of precipitous mountains, and the bad weather that comes to all those places.

For a long time Westerners have had a sense that we've largely mastered nature—that we've "subdued" the earth, as it says in Genesis. But I wonder whether our emotional relation to nature isn't changing, given concerns about climate change and fears that nature is out of balance, spinning off more and worse tropical storms, blizzards, and droughts. As Huxley points out, it's easy to love a "feeble and already conquered enemy," such as Wordsworth's defanged nature, but not "an unconquered, unconquerable, ceaselessly active enemy."

Vermont's Great Turkey Drives

November 24, 2010

Before railroads, the only way to get turkeys from Vermont to market in Boston was to walk them there. And that, throughout much of the nineteenth century, is exactly what Vermonters did, including Vermonters from the northern-most parts of the state. Townspeople put their birds of a feather together, and accompanied by wagons with camp supplies and tons of feed grain, they escorted as many as 7,000 birds at a time all the way to Boston. Drives of three to four thousand birds were common in the 1820s and '30s. Historian Charles Morrow Wilson says that about 1,000 birds was the minimum necessary to make the 150 to 350-mile trek worthwhile. It was a long haul. The flocks could make only ten to twelve miles a day, and at least one drover was required for each 100 birds.

Boys scattered shelled corn feed in front of the birds, so they would walk forward, while others herded from behind. Flocks might spread out for more than a mile, ranging in width from a few feet to fifty yards. To protect the birds' feet on such a long hike over rough terrain and November's frozen ground, Vermonters sometimes coated the birds' feet with warm tar. They lost about ten percent of the birds to forded rivers, fox, hungry farm families they met on route, and other perils of the journey.

Two key facts to keep in mind are: big birds, little brains. Wherever they were when the sun set, that's where they perched for the night. Their collective weight shattered trees. Occasionally, so many birds perched on a farmer's shed or barn that the building collapsed. They sometimes mistook the shade of a covered bridge for dusk and simply stopped. And so the drovers would have to go in, pick them up, carry them through the bridge and into the sun, where they'd perk up again and head on their way.

The advent of railroads and then, in the 1850s and '60s, refrigerated boxcars were the beginning of the end for the great turkey drives, but some lasted into the twentieth century. Now in the twenty-first century, the notion of driving thousands of turkeys, or even two birds on a leash, from Island Pond south all the way to Boston is charming in its absurdity.

Lilacs in the Dooryard

April 13, 2005

I've lived in a bunch of houses in New England, and every one has had a lilac bush out front. Lilacs are as much a part of New England homes as clapboards and chimneys. They've adorned northern door-yards for 250 years and made their way into our poetry as images of beauty, but also, interestingly, melancholy loss.

Lilacs are so hardy you'll still find them in the woods beside a cellar hole where a house stood two centuries ago, causing us to think of the poignant passage of time and the people, long dead, who once made their lives there. Writing in the early twentieth century, Vermont poet Daniel L. Cady begins his poem "An Old Vermont Cellar Hole" this way:

> To wander near a ruined home
>   Upon a Springtime morning,
> Informs the mind and charms the eye,
>   But gives the heart a warning;
> For, Oh! the sense of human change
>   That such a scene discloses—
> The roses 'round the fallen walls,
>   And lilacs 'round the roses.

The poem "Tide of Lilac" by Vermont poet Frances Frost (no relation to Robert Frost) is even more sentimental:

> From the Kennebec to Casco,
> from Lebanon to Dover,
> from Champlain to New Bedford,
> lilac has taken over.
>
> On roads to Narragansett,
> by Cornwall cellar holes,

the lilac spires are clustered
to plague New England souls.

Purple in clean-swept dooryards,
guarding the worn doorstones,
lilac invades the marrow
of reticent strong bones.

And careful housewives shiver,
and cautious men bite lips,
when they, with no one looking,
touch blue with their fingertips.

For Robert Frost, too, lilacs were associated with melancholy loss. In his poem "Directive," Frost describes the remains of a house in the woods and invites his reader to weep

...for the house that is no more a house,
But only a belilaced cellar hole,
Now slowly closing like a dent in dough.

For Walt Whitman, lilacs were inextricably linked in memory with the day Lincoln died, April 15, 1865. A year later, Whitman wrote,

When lilacs last in the dooryard bloom'd
And the great star early droop'd in the western sky in the night,
I mourn'd, and yet shall mourn with ever-returning spring.

Whitman continues,

In the dooryard fronting an old farm-house near the white-wash'd
palings,
Stands the lilac-bush tall-growing with heart-shaped leaves of rich
green,
With many a pointed blossom rising delicate, with the perfume
strong I love.

Perhaps Whitman associated lilacs with Lincoln's death so strongly because, scientists tell us, smell is the most evocative and memorable of the senses. But for us today, lilacs are unencumbered by such melancholy associations with the days that are no more, and their fragrance and beauty simply adorn our gardens and gladden our hearts in spring.

The Four Chaplains

October 13, 2003

O n a visit to our former hometown, Thetford, Vermont, I learned
something new about a town I thought I knew pretty well. In front
of the handsome brick Methodist church in town, right beside the Vil-
lage Store, is a new granite marker. It wasn't there when I was in town
last. I parked, walked over, and read the monument.

It honors four heroes of World War II who became known as the
Four Chaplains—two Protestant, one Roman Catholic, and one Jewish.
They became fast friends in chaplain school. Several months later, on
February 3, 1943, they died when their U.S. Army transport ship, the
Dorchester, was torpedoed in the North Atlantic. The ship went down
in less than thirty minutes. Of the 902 aboard, 672 were lost. After the
chaplains had distributed all the life vests available, they gave their
vests to others on board, and were last seen on deck, linked arm in arm
in prayer. One eyewitness recalled, "It was the finest thing I have ever
seen or hope to see this side of heaven."

Three years later, a postage stamp was issued honoring the Four
Chaplains and "interfaith action"; in 1960, Congress authorized a Special Medal for Heroism, which is never to be given again; and in Phila-
delphia, the Chapel of the Four Chaplains encourages "cooperation
and selfless service" and "unity without uniformity." In dedicating the
chapel in 1951, President Truman said "that as men can die heroically
as brothers so should they live together in mutual faith and good will."

The oldest of the four chaplains, Methodist minister George L. Fox,
was from Thetford. When America had entered World War I, he had
enlisted in the Marines at age seventeen. Standing just five feet seven
inches tall, he trained as an ambulance driver, and won a Silver Star for
rescuing a wounded soldier from a battlefield full of poisonous gas—
despite the fact that he had no gas mask. More than twenty years later,

after Pearl Harbor, Reverend Fox enlisted in the Army on the same day that his eighteen-year-old son Wyatt joined the Marines. Wyatt survived the war.

The story is a powerful, inspiring one. What an awakening it was for me to learn that from the gentle town of Thetford came this noble man. I wonder, were those four men exceptional, or were they, as it were, ordinary men who exhibited the exceptional potential that we all possess? Which would be a greater tribute to them—for them to be remembered as so heroic as to be made of different stuff than we, or as exemplars for us all, not of how to die, but how we might live? Perhaps that is what another clergyman, Reverend Martin Luther King, Jr., meant when he said, "Everybody can be great, because anybody can serve."

Memorial Day in Small Town America

May 25, 2007

The simple Memorial Day service in little Dorset, Vermont is profoundly moving for locals and visitors alike. All veterans, in uniform or not, are invited to enter the church with the color guard. The majority are World War II vets, now all over eighty, like my father. For many people, the most powerful part of the service is the recitation of the chronological honor roll—the names, dates, locations, and, where known, cause of death of the fifty-three Dorset residents who gave the last full measure of devotion. It's a poignant march through American history, and a powerful reminder of both the collective weight of sacrifice and the very personal cost—the fact that each casualty had a name and a face and a loving family, and a future cut short. It literally brings home the meaning of the day.

Of the fifty-three honored dead, one died in 1848 of yellow fever on his way home from the Mexican American War, thirty-six died in the Civil War, four in World War I, seven in World War II, two in Korea, and three in the Vietnam War. Of the thirty-six Civil War casualties, eleven were killed in action and twenty-five died of disease.

The Civil War casualties included:

Louis Chameau and Henry Heald, both killed June 29, 1862, Savages Station, Virginia;

Henry's brother Myron, who died of dysentery six months later in Pensacola, Florida;

Thomas Burns, killed July 3, 1864, Gettysburg, Pennsylvania;

Waldo Barrows and Horace Hill, both killed May 5, 1864, Battle of the Wilderness, Virginia;

Joshua Bromley, killed May 10, 1864, Spotsylvania, Virginia;

William Harwood, killed June 5, 1864, Cold Harbor, Virginia; and

Marquis Smith and Bela Fisher, killed in July and August
1864, Petersburg, Virginia.

In World War I three died of disease here in the States. And John Tuohy was killed in action September 29, 1918 on the Hindenburg Line in France. Then come the names of the fallen from the Second World War, Korea, and Vietnam, including, among others:

Myron Brophy, December 7, 1941, Pearl Harbor;

Horace Greeley Harwood, September 7, 1942 flying a Spitfire
from England;

Donald Tobin, January 19, 1945, Battle of the Bulge;

Clifton Baker, September 6, 1953, Korea;

Richard Thum, November 25, 1968, Vietnam; and

Allan Francis Wilkins, killed in a helicopter explosion, April 8,
1971 near Bien Hoa Air Force Base, Vietnam.

For me, Memorial Day is best understood in small-town America. It is the specifics of names and stories and the nexus between people and place that make one feel most keenly the power and import of casualty statistics and abstract statements about service and sacrifice.

Blue Willow Ware

May 25, 2010

When I was little, the two strongest associations with visits to my grandparents' house in southern Vermont were, first, the smells—especially the closet where they kept old toys—and, second, their blue Willow Ware dishes. To me they were the embodiment of age, both old people and bygone days.

You've probably seen Willow Ware countless times—white and cobalt blue dishes depicting a scene that includes several Chinese houses, a Chinese boat and bridge with three figures running across it, fruit trees, and, of course, a willow tree. It supposedly portrays a Chinese legend; in truth, the story's an English invention. It's a familiar kind of tale: a girl falls in love with a poor servant, but her wealthy and powerful father wants to marry her off to a rich old nobleman. The lovers elope; they are chased by the angry father. The old nobleman follows with his henchmen, the boy is slain, and the girl, in despair, sets fire to their house and perishes in the flames. But the pitying gods turn the lovers into immortal doves, to dwell in beauty and constancy. You can see the birds on the plates flying above their former earthly dwellings.

I didn't know it as a child, of course, but Willow Ware is the most common plate design in English history; it was especially popular during the Victorian era. The pattern originated in 1780 at a porcelain factory in Shropshire; soon countless manufacturers were making it. It was so well known that it appeared in many Victorian plays and novels. Indeed, it's central to the theme of a masterful 1879 novel entitled *The Egoist,* by George Meredith. Although the plot doesn't follow the Chinese legend verbatim, the novel depicts the difficulties of being a woman in English society, where too often fathers and suitors looked at a bride as a commodity—as in the Chinese story.

The Egoist (or "Egg-oist," as the English would say) is the story of the self-absorbed and controlling Sir Willoughby Patterne. (Get it? Sir Willow-bee Pattern!) His attempts to marry several different women, including the heroine, meet with no success. At one point, the independent-minded heroine is described as "a dainty rogue in porcelain." When the Egoist asks why she's "a rogue," he's told enigmatically, "Porcelain explains it"—an allusion to the strong-willed girl in the Willow Ware legend. The allusion is lost on Sir Willoughby Patterne, but not on careful readers!

After the novel was published, a friend of George Meredith's came to him terribly upset: he thought that Meredith had modeled the character Willoughby Patterne after him. "This is too bad of you," he cried. "Willoughby is me!"

"No, my dear fellow," said the author; "He is all of us."

And so Meredith, with his ingenious analogy between the Willow Ware legend depicting traditional Chinese culture and his social satire of Victorian English society, successfully interpreted a foreign-sounding tale and a popular plate pattern in a way that makes *both* resonate, even today, with men and women alike.

All that Stuff

October 1, 2003

Anyone who has moved knows what an astonishing amount of stuff we accumulate even without being particularly acquisitive. The days are long past when I could pack everything into a Volkswagen. When we moved last, we got rid of hundreds of beloved books, held a yard sale, and took multiple loads to Goodwill and the dump. And still what a lot of stuff we moved!

We are not a materialistic family, and yet it is important to remain alert to the issue. The Catholic social worker Peter Maurin, colleague of Dorothy Day, used to say, "The coat in the closet belongs to the poor." Lord knows, I have more than one coat in the closet.

A stunning photography book entitled *Material World* captures families around the world in front of their homes with all their worldly possessions. In some countries, a large family stands before a hut with a few pots and bedrolls. In other photos, many more objects accompany people on their life's journey, just as pharaohs were buried with treasures to accompany them to the next world. My American family would need a wide-angle lens, even after the yard sale.

I think also of a children's book called *The Donkey Prince*, M. Jean Craig's adaptation of a Grimm fairy tale, illustrated by Barbara Cooney. It's the story of a king and queen who have everything they could want except a child. When their son arrives, he's a donkey because they tried to shortchange the wizard who had helped them. I read it numerous times to our young daughters before I was struck by its first pages: on one page is an illustration of a medieval king who resembles Henry VIII counting gold coins, and on the opposite page, his queen gazes in a mirror while maids dress her.

The book says, "The King loved nothing better than his riches. He spent most of his time in his strongroom, counting silver bars and golden coins and bags of rubies and pearls. The Queen loved nothing better than pretty clothes. She spent most of her time before her mirror, trying on gowns and robes, collars and capes, feathers and silks and furs."

Setting aside the gender stereotyping, the medieval setting had blinded me to the fact that we often spend our lives like this today. How much time do we spend shopping as a pastime, rather than because we need something? How many of us spend too-long hours at work making and counting our money?

Traditionally, Vermonters have done pretty well in this area: there's the old joke about the woman from the city who asks, "It's so lovely up here in Vermont, but where do you buy your clothes?" And the Vermonter replies, "We have our clothes." But we have to stay attentive. Materialism and covetousness are less likely to appear to us in the repugnant guise of Imelda Marcos's shoe closet than as our favorite shopping catalogue.

It's Not about the Beans

August 29, 2007

L ike many families, mine has had an annual reunion each summer for many, many years. For the last thirty-seven years, they've taken on a specific form and ritual that seems to bind us together and contribute to making the occasion feel more special. The event is called the Bean Hole.

Every August on a Saturday, fifty to seventy-five of us gather after supper at a cousin's home in southern Vermont. We light a carefully stacked campfire tower of maple and ash three feet tall. When the fire eventually collapses in on itself, the embers fall into a hole dug in the ground. A heavy Dutch oven full of baked beans is then lowered into the hole, covered with hot coals, and buried overnight. Then it's time for the kids to toast marshmallows and make s'mores.

The next day, in the afternoon, we gather again, and with great mock ceremony, dig up the beans; the Chief Bean opens the pot of beans, tastes them, and, each year, declares them, "Better than ever."

Then comes a potluck supper, with homemade strawberry ice cream, made by the Queen Bean. A senior member of the family, "the family genealogist," makes brief remarks about family history. A cousin gives out awards, including Green Bean awards for people attending their first Bean Hole. Five-year olds help by delivering the tokens to the recipients. Then comes an auction of family-related objects, things you don't want but perhaps someone else might—a cane that was cousin Alfred's, or a painting by cousin Janet. Sometimes there's music or other activity. One year, the Chief Bean at the time, a retired philosophy professor who had become interested in Tai Chi, led the young kids in Vermont Tai Chi, four exercises that corresponded to the seasons. The winter exercise looked a lot like someone shoveling snow in very slow motion; spring bore an uncanny resemblance to waving black flies away.

We peruse photo albums from previous years' gatherings, and see just how much younger we were then. Each year someone makes a small commemorative banner, and they're all displayed on a clothesline strung between the barn and an old maple tree. Most of the banners have something to do with beans. For example, the banner from 1997, the year that the comet Hale Bopp came close to Earth, shows a flaming comet shaped like a baked bean. Many banners incorporate figures that symbolize family members who had passed away that year— a rooster, for example, to honor Frederick, who had raised chickens with his brother.

Despite all the hoopla about burying the beans and digging them up, of course it's really not about the beans at all. It's about connectedness, family, and fun. And the tradition and ritual, silly as they may be, are the frame and glue that help it happen.

Vermont's Reel History on Ice

March 22, 2010

In March 1920, director D.W. Griffith shot the climactic scenes of his classic silent movie *Way Down East,* starring Lillian Gish. It's a melodrama about Anna, a poor country girl who's tricked into a fake wedding. She becomes pregnant, the baby dies, and she wanders the countryside until she finds employment with Squire Bartlett. But, when the town gossip tells the Squire about Anna's past, he throws her out into a raging blizzard. She becomes lost in the storm and falls unconscious on the river ice, which breaks up, sending her downstream toward the falls.

Even if you haven't seen the movie, you may be familiar with the thrilling scene in which Anna is rescued from the ice floe just as she's about to go over the falls. It's been called "one of the most remarkable sequences in film history probably containing the single most memorable images of the silent screen." And it was filmed in Hartford, Vermont, on both the White River and the Connecticut River. The filmmakers used dynamite upstream to break up the river ice and create the large chunks for the heroine to float on, unconscious, and for the hero (who is the Squire's loving son) to leap across to save her just in time.

Making the film was cold work. Griffith's crew built fires under the camera tripods to stop the movie cameras from freezing. It was Gish herself who suggested to her director that she trail her hand and hair in the water as she floated downstream on the ice floe. Griffith loved the effect. Gish may have regretted it—after a while, her hair froze, and her hand felt as if it were in a flame. "When the sequence was finally finished," she recalled, "I had been on a slab of ice at least twenty times a day for three weeks. In between takes, one of the men would throw a coat around me, and I would warm myself briefly at a fire."

The story was originally a play that was hugely popular in the late 1800s. Griffith bought the film rights. The river ice sequence wasn't even in the play; the scene, by far the most memorable aspect of the film, was added by Griffith, probably inspired by a similar sequence in another hugely successful melodrama, Harriet Beecher Stowe's anti-slavery novel, *Uncle Tom's Cabin*.

Yes, it's melodrama, but it's good melodrama. Not surprisingly, it is moralistic and dated in some ways, but I found the two and a half hour film remarkably engaging. I enjoyed it in part just for its portrayal of early twentieth century rural New England. It really is a classic, right from Hartford, Vermont, where, D. W. Griffith graciously told the townspeople, he had found "the real backbone of Americanism."

Steve Martin's *Shopgirl*

July 17, 2006

I recently saw the movie *Shopgirl*, starring Steve Martin. He also wrote the screenplay and the book upon which the movie is based. The movie is rated R; it might be called a romantic comedy, but it is bittersweet.

In one scene a gold digger in Los Angeles advises another young woman how she can snare a rich guy under false (and indecent) pretenses. But the nice shopgirl, the film's heroine, says, "I couldn't do all that."

"How come?"

"I'm from Vermont," she replies.

The line gets cheers and applause in Vermont theaters. When the shopgirl says she's from Vermont, the author is using shorthand to say that she has certain values—admirable values, like decency, a recognition that money isn't everything, and, above all, honesty. Isn't it nice that our state is associated nationwide with honesty?

When I was a kid, I remember my mother going into a hardware store in Manchester. She told the man she needed fifty-two yards of webbing to replace the old webbing on aluminum folding lawn chairs. The salesman took down a huge roll and began to measure it off. Then he stopped, and handing her the whole roll, said, "Here. When you bring it back, tell us how much you've used."

My mother was surprised. She thanked them, and then added as an afterthought, "Don't you want to know who I am?"

The salesman replied, "You're going to bring it back, aren't you?"

We've all been to Vermont farm stands that have a coffee can or cigar box where you leave your money. More cautious farm stands have a sign that says, "Please put your money in the slot in the door." At least that way a person could, I suppose, walk off with the sweet corn and tomatoes, but not the cash from the till. Not too long ago, I saw a sign in a public building in St. Albans that said, "Soda is $.75 a can. Put money in Cool Whip bowl on top of refrigerator."

The survey of the quality of life conducted by the Vermont Business Roundtable in 2005 reported that 71 percent of Vermonters say that most people in Vermont can be trusted, compared with just 34 percent in national polls.

I don't know if Vermonters are any more honest than anyone else. But I like to think so, in part out of pride, I suppose, and in part because to a certain degree, it's a self-fulfilling prophecy: If you think people are honest, you're more likely to be honest, too; if you trust people, people are more likely to trust you. Of course, we all should know that if you trust people, sooner or later, you're going to get burned; that's just the way it is. We have to decide whether, knowing that, we'll keep trusting. I think that reasonable trust, like love, is worth the risk. Because being trusted and trusting others contributes to one's quality of life, even if you are disappointed now and again.

The St. Johnsbury Athenaeum

March 31, 2004

A thenaeum. It's a word from another era. It originally meant a temple of Athena, the goddess of wisdom, where poets, philosophers, and rhetoricians met. An athenaeum these days is a library, literary club, or other institution dedicated to the promotion of learning; a place where the arts and humanities, reading and learning, are part of everyday life and central to a vigorous civic culture.

The St. Johnsbury Athenaeum is one of the legacies of Horace Fairbanks, who made his fortune manufacturing his invention, the platform scale. Some athenaeums were and still are private, open only to members. Not the St. Johnsbury Athenaeum: Mr. Fairbanks gave it to his hometown, and it unites the dignity of a nineteenth-century men's club with the openness and warmth of a vital, modern library in democratic America. Everyone is welcome, and, in fact, everyone visits, including adults of all backgrounds, teenagers, and young kids. The Athenaeum is a visible and outward manifestation of, well, the humanities in Vermont. It's been called "a monument to the nineteenth-century belief in learning."

Built in 1871, the Athenaeum has not only undergone a thorough renovation; it now boasts new, Victorian-style skylights made of high-tech triple-pane glass that protect the nineteenth-century art gallery's prize collection of paintings and furnishings from the sun's harmful UV rays. Gone is the former wall-to-wall carpet; beneath your feet now are hardwood floors of alternating light and dark wood, ash and walnut. Magnificent paintings in gilded frames abound, including one of Yosemite Valley by Albert Bierstadt that covers an entire wall. Wooden spiral staircases, oak bookcases, and paneling virtually glow.

In the main room on the second floor, site of public talks and poetry readings, a drop ceiling has been removed to reveal a stunning painted ceiling and tall, arched windows. The space takes your breath away. Indeed I thought of Emily Dickinson's definition of poetry. "If," she wrote, when she is reading a book, "I feel physically as if the top of my head were taken off, I know this is poetry." That's the way I felt in that lofty room—as if the top of my head were taken off. The St. Johnsbury Athenaeum is poetry, in brick and wood.

With the elegant French Second Empire-style building now restored, refurbished, and wired for the information age, the St. Johnsbury Athenaeum is a sturdy testimonial to the ongoing capacity of the past, learning, and excellence to inspire and teach. It's an elegant statement in brick about the power of art and ideas, or "beauty and truth," as Keats wrote in his poem "Ode on a Grecian Urn."

The St. Johnsbury Athenaeum is not only worth seeing, it is worth going to see—even going a long way to see. Check it out, and check out some of the books while you're at it.

A Summer Inspired by Wordsworth

August 20, 2003

Some years ago, my two young daughters and I camped out on the side of Mount Mansfield. We built a fire, which they tended constantly with the joyous excitement of youth. We made s'mores and watched the sky's light slowly fade over the Adirondacks and the silver mirror that was Lake Champlain.

The next morning, they wanted to explore the stream. In soggy sneakers, we walked up the middle of the streambed, wading through its chilly pools, stepping from boulder to boulder, climbing over fallen logs, and skirting, undisturbed, a perfect miniature waterfall between rocks mottled with white quartz and wrapped with rich green moss. That, they said, was their favorite spot. I knew, if they didn't, that in the words of the poet William Wordsworth, "in this moment there is life and food/For future years."

The line comes from Wordsworth's poem "Tintern Abbey," which captures his thoughts upon revisiting the banks of a small river; it was a place of natural and pastoral beauty that he had visited many times when young. He writes that he owed to his boyhood memories of that scene "sensations sweet":

> ... feelings too
> Of unremembered pleasure: such, perhaps,
> As have no slight or trivial influence
> On that best portion of a good man's life,
> His little, nameless, unremembered acts
> Of kindness and of love.

The place I remember like that from my childhood is the Merck Forest in Rupert, Vermont. It, like our campsite on Mount Mansfield, boasts a view toward New York state that is, as they say in Brooklyn, "to die for." When I was a boy in the 1960s, we'd go up to the Merck Place for family cookouts.

One evening, with great uncles and aunts, cousins and kin galore, we went past our usual cookout spot and up Antone Mountain to a place where there had been a beaver pond. The dam had failed, leaving the pond empty and the beaver lodge high and dry. I was small enough to be able to crawl on my stomach up the rising tunnel and into the abandoned lodge. What a thrilling place—a kind of igloo of stick and mud animated by a boy's love of nature and an imagination inspired by *The Wind in the Willows* and *Mother West Wind's Children*. Never have I felt more thrilled, or more closely linked to the natural world. Alice had fallen down the rabbit hole, but I had crawled up into a beaver lodge to find a treasure chamber of gnawed sticks and dried mud.

With age, Wordsworth's view on nature changed, and so has mine. The "wild ecstasies" of youth have "matured/Into a sober pleasure." But I have no doubt that by exposing our girls to the natural world and to the words that nature has inspired, they will gain not only years of joy, but also, as Wordsworth asserted, a kind of personal resilience that comes from faith, rootedness, and serenity.